EXAMINING THE GENETIC RELATIONSHIP OF BINUKID LANGUAGE VARIETIES

EXAMINING THE GENETIC RELATIONSHIP OF BINUKID LANGUAGE VARIETIES

Dickson P. Pagente
Mary Ann E. Tarusan

GALDA VERLAG 2022

Bibliografische Information der Deutschen Nationalbibliothek
Die Deutsche Nationalbibliothek verzeichnet diese Publikation in der Deutschen Nationalbibliografie; detaillierte bibliografische Daten sind im Internet über https://dnb.de abrufbar.

© 2022 Galda Verlag, Glienicke
Neither this book nor any part may be reproduced or transmitted in any form or by any means electronic or mechanical, including photocopying, micro-filming, and recording, or by any information storage or retrieval system, without prior permission in writing from the publisher. Direct all inquiries to:
Galda Verlag, Franz-Schubert-Str. 61, 16548 Glienicke, Germany

Originally presented as Dickson Pagente's doctoral thesis at Central Mindanao University, University Town, Musuan, Bukidnon, Philippines, 2019

ISBN 978-3-96203-251-7 (Print)
ISBN 978-3-96203-252-4 (E-Book)

ACKNOWLEDGMENT

This study would not have been possible without the Almighty God – the source of all my blessings, strength, energy, wisdom, and intelligence. Thank you, Lord, for providing all my necessities, for giving me good health, and for protecting me from any unfavorable circumstances throughout this journey.

To the Commission on Higher Education (CHED), thank you for giving me this opportunity to pursue my doctorate studies in applied linguistics as a scholar. Without this scholarship, I would have not been very motivated to go beyond my limits.

To my family, my Papa Ani who is now in heaven, my Mama Omit, my siblings, nephews, nieces, and friends back at home, thank you for all the support in all the things that I want to do and achieve in life. You have been at my back ever since this journey began.

To SAIT, thank you so much for being my second home. Special thanks to the former school president, Sr. Virginia A. Loquias, MCM and the former finance officer, Sr. Serina T. Maraveles, MCM. Of course, thank you to the present school president, Sr. Gina L. Dahan, MCM and the present finance officer, Sr. Elizabeth U. Bag-ao, MCM for the financial and moral support.

To Dr. Aida C. Selecios, our former dean, for nominating us to this CHED Scholarship. You are one of the biggest reasons in the fulfillment of this dream. Thank you as well to Dr. Glenne A. Rivera, our present dean for the constant support in all our undertakings.

Special thanks to Maam Lory for the motherly presence and Julsar for the brotherly care, and for being my best buddies in the achievement of this dream. I cannot forget the days we spent in travelling to Davao City back and forth.

To all the experts and research authorities who have contributed a lot for the refinement of this study. These include my dissertation adviser, Dr. Mary Ann E. Tarusan, my editor Dr. Jerlyn G. Balones, my internal validators, my external validator, Dr. Teresita D. Borres of Central Mindanao University, my data analysts, Dr. Riceli C. Mendoza of the University of Southern Mindanao and Sir Eric W. Holman of the University of California, Los Angeles, my dissertation professor, Dr. Gloria P. Gempes, the Research Coordinator of the

Professional schools of the University of Mindanao, Dr. Ana Helena R. Lovitos, the members of the panel, Dr. Jocelyn B. Bacasmot, Dr. Riceli C. Mendoza, and Dr. Benedict V. Omblero, the members of the University of Mindanao Ethics Review Committee (UMERC), and the Office of Quality Control.

To all my classmates: Claire, Alfel, Ahah, Steve, Jeyz, Marlon, Melody, Philip, Maam Che, Maam Lolit, Maam Dodong, Maam Edna, and Maam Ping, thank you so much for making memories that are very enjoyable. Though we struggled for so many times, hand in hand, we are still able to persevere and reach the finish line. Thank you for the tears and laughter because these made us even stronger.

The cooperation of the barangay captains of Sumilao, Kibangay, and Casisang, Bukidnon, gatekeepers, and the voluntary participation of the participants deserve to be acknowledged as well. Without all of them, I would not be able to finish this study successfully. Thank you so much.

D.P.P.

ABSTRACT

This study examined the genetic relationship of the three Binukid language varieties namely Higaonon Binukid, Talaandig Binukid, and Bukidnon Binukid. These three Binukid varieties are particularly spoken by the Higaonon, Talaandig, and Bukidnon tribal groups in the province of Bukidnon. Knowing the genetic relationship of these three Binukid varieties will shed light to the present inconsistencies about the Binukid language. Employing the instrumental case study design, this study explored the socio-demographic profile of the informants in terms of age, dialect spoken, other languages spoken, and highest educational attainment; and, the genetic relationship of the three Binukid language varieties spoken by the Higaonon, Talaandig, and Bukidnon tribes by examining the phonological variations and correspondences of these three Binukid varieties; the percentage of genetic relationship of these Binukid varieties when examined using the ASJP software; the time depth of these Binukid varieties; and the phylogenetic classification of these language varieties. By examining the phonological variations and sound correspondences of the three Binukid varieties and with the use of the Automated Similarity Judgment Program (ASJP), the study revealed that these three Binukid varieties are genetically related with Higaonon and Bukidnon Binukid varieties as the most similar pairs gaining 98.61 percent similarity in Swadesh 100 Wordlist and 97.56 percent similarity in Swadesh 40 Wordlist. Meanwhile, Higaonon and Talaandig Binukid varieties the same with Talaandig and Bukidnon varieties gradually split from each other in the past 48 years as of the moment of this writing. This implies that Talaandig Binukid variety branched off first from the other two varieties in the past 48 years. This divergence was illustrated in a language tree at the end of the study.

Keywords: *historical linguistics, lexicostatistics, genetic relationship, Binukid language, Automated Similarity Judgment Program (ASJP), Philippines*

TABLE OF CONTENTS

Acknowledgment	i
Abstract	iii

CHAPTER 1

INTRODUCTION	**1**
Rationale of the Study	1
Purpose of the Study	2
Research Questions	3
Theoretical Lens	3
Significance of the Study	4
Definition of Terms	5
Limitation and Delimitation	6
Organization of the Study	7

CHAPTER 2

REVIEW OF RELATED LITERATURE	**9**
The Current Scenario	9
Socio–Demographic Profile	10
Genetic Relationship of Languages and Language Divergence	12
The Higaonon, Talaandig, and Bukidnon Binukid Varieties	13
Phonetic Variations and Sound Correspondences	14
Lexicostatistics, Glottochronology, and ASJP	15
Classical Methodology using Lexicostatistics	16
Related Studies Employing Classical Lexicostatistics	19
Contemporary Methodology on Lexicostatistics	22
Doing Lexicostatistics using ASJP	22
Related Lexicostatistical Studies that Employ ASJP	24

CHAPTER 3

METHODOLOGY — 27

- Research Design — 27
- Role of the Researcher — 28
- Research Participants — 28
- Research Materials — 29
- Data Collection — 29
- Data Analysis — 31
- Trustworthiness — 31
- Ethical Consideration — 33

CHAPTER 4

RESULTS — 39

- The Socio-Demographic Profile of the Informants — 39
- The Genetic Relationship of the Three Binukid Language Varieties — 41
- The Time-Depth (Year of Divergence) of these Language Varieties — 49
- The Phylogenetic Classification of these Language Varieties — 50

CHAPTER 5

DISCUSSION — 55

- The Socio–Demographic Profile of the Informants — 56
- Genetic Relationship of the Higaonon, Talaandig, and Bukidnon Binukid Varieties — 58
- Time-Depth or Language Divergence of the Higaonon, Talaandig, and Bukidnon Binukid Varieties — 60
- The Phylogenetic Classification of the Higaonon, Talaandig, and Bukidnon Binukid Varieties — 61
- Implications for Practice — 63
- Implications for Future Research — 64
- Concluding Remarks — 65

References — 67

CHAPTER 1
INTRODUCTION

This chapter presents the rationale of the study, purpose of the study, research questions, theoretical lens, significance of the study, definition of terms, limitation and delimitation, and organization of the study.

Rationale of the Study

Binukid is an ethnic language known to be spoken by the original tribal inhabitants in Bukidnon. Three particular ethnic groups that are known to speak Binukid are the Higaonon, Talaandig, and the Bukidnon as classified by the Presidential Assistant for National Minorities (PANAMIN) in 1970s based on geographical locations (Industan, 2009; Thomas, 2000). Accordingly, these Binukid speakers slightly differ in their dialects and have more language affinities in their speech. However, inconsistency existed between the reports in PANAMIN and Elkins (1974). The former identified three Binukid speaking tribes such as Higaonon, Talaandig, and Bukidnon while the latter reported that Binukid is only spoken by the Higaonon and Talaandig tribes. Suminguit, Burton, and Canoy (2001) even stressed that it is ambiguous whether these three ethnic groups are distinct from each other or just one tribal group with three different names.

For more than a century, the government and the people of Bukidnon persistently clung to the common belief that these language varieties share linguistic commonalities. However, Elkins (1974), an influential linguist, recognized only Higaonon and Talaandig tribes as Binukid speakers dropping Bukidnon as non–Binukid speakers. For me, as the researcher, the conduct of this study is important since it will enlighten and clarify inconsistencies on the report of these language varieties. This study may interweave these inconsistencies to give real identities of these language varieties.

Furthermore, after these inconsistencies are solved, I believe this study will, in either way, contribute to the strengthening of the common belief that these Binukid languages are real varieties or reject the common belief that one of these three Binukid varieties is not a real Binukid variety at all. In a broader sense, this study give identities to these languages spoken by the Higaonon, Talaandig, and Bukidnon tribes. The findings of this study will become a useful reference for future language policy making and the efforts for language preservation.

Finally, one issue that this research attempts to address is the "insufficiency of studies (particularly lexicostatistical or genetic relationship studies) on these Binukid varieties". There are related studies available but these are mostly authored by foreign researchers. Moreover, their researches are on a large scale dealing on the Austronesian group of languages (Dyen, 1962) and the subgrouping of Philippine languages (Thomas & Healy, 1962). On the other hand, one study applied lexicostatistics in the historical development of three languages in the Philippines but these languages are inclusive to Tagalog, Ilokano, and Bikolano only (Nelson, 2001). In other words, the present researcher has not found a lexicostatistical study on the three Binukid varieties. Thus, a research gap exists.

Given the abovementioned premises, the present researcher is motivated to explore on the genetic relationship among these three Binukid varieties to contribute to the body of linguistic literature and fill in the existing research gap.

Purpose of the Study

This study is exploratory and confirmatory by nature since it attempts to explore the genetic relationship of the three Binukid varieties in Bukidnon and confirms whether one variety is a real Binukid variety or not at all. To know the genetic relationship of these three Binukid varieties, I asked help from Eric W. Holman, a professor from the University of California and one of the eight scholars (psychologists, linguists and anthropologists) who created the Automated Similarity Judgment Program (ASJP), a software designed through rigid logarithms to examine genetic relationship of the languages in the world.

Further, through this study, I, as the researcher want to determine the time depth of these languages. In other words, the time when these varieties diverged (separated) from each other. After knowing the genetic relationship and time depth of these varieties, I would be able to construct a phylogenetic classification or basically a language tree of these varieties.

Finally, in a broader perspective, the main purpose of this study is to give enlightenment and clarification to the present inconsistencies on the reports of these Binukid language varieties. With this, I would be able to confirm existing facts or even correct erroneous reports about the relationship of these Binukid language varieties.

Research Questions

1. What is the socio-demographic profile of the informants in terms of: age, dialect spoken, other languages spoken, and highest educational attainment?
2. How are the three Binukid language varieties spoken by the Higaonon, Talaandig, and Bukidnon tribes genetically related?
   - 2.1 What are the phonological variations and correspondences of these three Binukid varieties?
   - 2.2 What is the percentage of genetic relationship of these Binukid varieties when examined using the ASJP software?
   - 2.3 What is the time depth of these Binukid varieties?
   - 2.4 What is the phylogenetic classification of these language varieties?

Theoretical Lens

The Proto–Manobo Theory by Elkins (1974) and Swadesh's Assumptions on Lexicostatistics (Gudschinsky, 1956; Swadesh, 1952) are used as the theoretical lens of this study.

The term Proto–Manobo was coined to describe the stock of aboriginal non–Negritoid people of Mindanao who are commonly known as "Manobo". Elkins (1974) refers Manobo as the speakers of certain Philippine languages which constitute a Manobo subgroup within the Philippine subfamily. This subgroup consists of twelve daughter languages that includes Tigwa Manobo, Sarangani Manobo, Western Bukidnon Manobo, Ilianen Manobo, Dibabawon Manobo, Cotabato Manobo, Tasaday, Cagayano of Cagayancillo Island, Kinamigin of Camiguin Island, Tagabawa and Obo of Mt. Apo region in Davao Province, and the Binukid speakers particularly in Bukidnon. In addition, the Proto–Manobo Theory suggests that Binukid, together with Kinamigin and Cagayano are under the North Manobo subgrouping.

Since Elkins (1974) recognized Higaonon and Talaandig only as the Binukid speaking tribes in Bukidnon, it is in this gap that I intended to examine whether Bukidnon, as claimed by them is another Binukid speaking ethnic group in the province (although the four other ethnic groups in Bukidnon claimed to speak Binukid as well which of course entails further research).

Moreover, this study is anchored on the assumptions of Swadesh (1952) on lexicostatistics, a method developed by Swadesh in 1950s to help language researchers examine the relationship between two or more languages by determining the percentage of lexical similarity of these languages. Swadesh (1952) proposed a wordlist composed of core vocabularies that are assumed to be the most stable words in a language. In historical linguistics studies, these core vocabularies are to be translated in the target languages to come up with cognates in these languages. To encapsulate, lexicostatistics is used to determine genetic relationship, time depth or language divergence, and, subgrouping or phylogenetic classification (Nelson, 2001).

Lexicostatistics is founded on four basic assumptions: first, some vocabularies of any language are more resistant to change. These vocabularies are assumed to be more stable that the meaning of these words remain the same through time (Swadesh, 1952). These vocabularies were classified by Bowern (2015) into pronouns, quantity, adjective, human noun, animal, environment, animal product, body part, body verb, perception verb, impact, motion, transfer, color, and time.

From this standpoint, the premise above provides an overview on the second basic assumption of lexicostatistics which states that these core vocabularies' rate of retention in the language is constant across millennia. That is, a percentage of these words will remain in the language millennium after millennium of vocabulary loss. Further, the third basic assumption is that all languages share approximately the same rate of lexical loss which is attributed to language contact between and among linguistic groups.

Finally, the fourth assumption of lexicostatistics is that, time (in years) that has elapsed when two languages split or diverged from a parent language can be computed given that cognates are already identified in these languages provided that the divergence of these languages is not interfered by movements of people, invasions, and language contact (Gudschinsky, 1955; Lees, 1953; Swadesh, 1950).

Significance of the Study

In a global perspective, this study is significant to linguists, historians, and anthropologists alike since this study will potentially give them an ample data on the genetic relationship of the Binukid varieties as spoken by the Higa-onon, Talaandig, and Bukidnon tribes in Bukidnon. In fact, the result of this study would become an important contribution to the ASJP (Automated

Similarity Judgment Program) Database created by Wichmann et al. (2010) which aims to contain a 40–item wordlist of all the world's languages which will be used to classify language groups and infer language divergence.

Moreover, the result of this study would be a great contribution to the inadequate body of literature about the Binukid language varieties and the tribes that speak of it. In this way, the Binukid language will be valued as an important ethnic language in the province of Bukidnon. Integral government programs might be formed then to preserve this language. In the social aspect, the Binukid speakers in the province will also be valued as important contributors to the development and maintenance of the language and for enriching the cultural heritage of the province of Bukidnon.

Further, this study might make a good resource material as this would establish a fact by either confirming that the language spoken by the Bukidnon tribe is a variety of the Binukid spoken by the Higaonon and Talaandig tribes. By establishing either of this fact, I will be able to correct inconsistencies on the reports about the Binukid language which will eventually cascade to the corrections of textbooks, educational materials, and even research articles about the language. All of these become beneficial to the provincial government of Bukidnon and the future researchers of the Binukid language.

Definition of Terms

The following terms are defined conceptually or operationally for a better understanding of this study:

Binukid - It is an ethnic language spoken in the north–central part of Mindanao particularly in Bukidnon, Misamis Oriental, Agusan del Norte, Agusan del Sur, and some parts of Cotabato. In terms of phylogeny, Binukid is considered to be part of the following subgroups of Austronesian, in descending order: Malayo-Polynesian; Greater Central Philippines; Manobo; and, North Manobo (Elkins, 1974; Peng & Billings, 2008). Binukid is spoken by the Higaonon, Talaandig, and Bukidnon tribes as classified by PANAMIN in the report of Thomas (2000) and Industan (2009) while Elkins (1974) in Ethnologue claimed that Binukid is spoken only by the Higaonon and Talaandig tribes. What makes it more interesting is that, the other four tribes in Bukidnon also claimed to be speaking Binukid which calls for further research in the future.

Genetic Relationship - In linguistics, it refers to the degree of 'relatedness' of two or more languages. Languages that have genetic relationship are descendants from a parent language. For example, Spanish and Italian are genetically related languages with Latin as their parent language. In classical lexicostatistics, cognates from the languages compared are examined in its phonetic similarities. When a certain percentage is established, one can say that the languages under study are genetically related or not. This percentage can also be used to determine time depth which means the time when these languages separated from their parent language. In this study however, Binukid language varieties spoken by the Higaonon, Talaandig, and Bukidnon tribes will be examined in its genetic relationship through a contemporary methodology using a software called Automated Similarity Judgement Program (ASJP).

Limitation and Delimitation

This study focused only on examining the genetic relationship among the 'Binukid' varieties spoken by Talaandig, Higa-onon, and Bukidnon tribes in Bukidnon. Furthermore, it sought to examine the time depth or the point when these varieties diverged from one another. Hence, at the end of the study, a phylogenetic classification of these languages were formed.

It must be noted that this study did not include the other four tribes in Bukidnon that include Manobo, Matigsalug, Umayamnon, and Tigwahanon though these tribes claimed to be Binukid speakers as well. Hence, further research to validate this claim is needed in the future.

Furthermore, the findings of this study will give clarification and enlightenment to the real identities of these Binukid varieties whether these are real varieties or one is not a variety of the other. Establishing this fact is beneficial to the national and provincial government and to the academic community particularly in Bukidnon since inconsistencies of reports will be corrected and solved.

Meanwhile, one possible weakness or limitation of this study is language contamination. Since the informants are already exposed to second languages like Cebuano, English, and Filipino, accuracy on the translation of the Swadesh wordlist might be affected.

Lastly, this study did not directly promote programs for language preservation since it never addressed language loss or death of the Binukid language. Though, officials may refer to the findings of the study for possible policy making.

Organization of the Study

This study is organized into four chapters excluding the preliminary and final pages. Preliminary pages include the title page, approval sheet, acknowledgment, abstract, table of contents, and list of tables. On the other hand, final pages include the references, appendices, and the curriculum vitae of the researcher.

Chapter 1 focuses on the problem situation which in this study is the inconsistency on the report of the Binukid language by Industan (2009), in PANAMIN as reported by Thomas (2000) and Elkins (1974). Specifically, this chapter presents the introduction of the study which subdivided into rationale, purpose of the study, research questions, theoretical lens, significance of the study, definitions of terms, delimitations and limitations, and organization of the study.

Meanwhile, Chapter 2 mainly deals on the review of related literature of the study. Specifically, this chapter presents the current scenario regarding the inconsistency of reports on the Binukid language, the Higaonon, Talaandig, and Bukidnon tribes, genetic relationship, discussion on genetic relationship, lexicostatistics and glottochronology, classical methodology using lexicostatistics, related studies on classical lexicostatistics, contemporary methodology on lexicostatistics, doing lexicostatistics using ASJP, related lexicostatistical studies that employ ASJP.

Chapter 3 comprises the methodology of the study which include the research design, role of the researcher, research participants, research materials, data collection, data analysis, trustworthiness, and ethical consideration.

Lastly, Chapter 4 presents the result and Chapter 5 presents the discussion on the result, implication for practice, implication for future research, and the concluding remarks.

CHAPTER 2
REVIEW OF RELATED LITERATURE

Presented in this chapter is the review of related literature and studies that have significant bearing on the present study.

The Current Scenario

As mentioned in the previous chapter, there is an inconsistency on the records about the ethnic groups who originally inhabited Bukidnon and their languages. Bukidnon history dictates that there are seven tribes that settled in the province of which Higaonon, Talaandig, and Bukidnon are just three of these seven. This historical fact is even articulated on the provincial government website.

It is a common knowledge then by the people of Bukidnon that these seven ethnic groups speak Binukid. In fact, these tribal groups in the province would also claim that they too speak Binukid. Until, the now–defunct PANAMIN and Industan (2009), an academician and a native Bukidnon classified the Binukid into three varieties which accordingly is spoken by the Higaonon, Talaandig, and the Bukidnon tribes. Meanwhile, the other four tribal groups were never mentioned by these authorities to be Binukid speakers.

On the contrary, Elkins (1974) in his glottochronological works reported that Binukid is only spoken by the Higaonon and Talaandig tribes which simply implies that Bukidnon tribe is not a Binukid–speaking group. This report of Elkins even rejected the common belief of Bukidnon citizens and the claim of the four other remaining tribes that Binukid is spoken by all seven tribes.

What makes it more confusing is that the Bukidnon provincial government website stated that Binukid is the dialect of the Bukidnon tribal group but never stated that the same Binukid is spoken by the Higaonon and Talaandig tribal groups. The website does not even mention that Binukid is also spoken by the remaining four tribal groups in the province. This contrasting fact leaves a big question to me as the present researcher as to what tribal group really speaks Binukid.

Furthermore, SIL International presented linguistic data that adds up to the existing inconsistency. Ethnologue, a project by SIL International, presented that Binukid is a sister language of Higaonon, Kagayanen, and Manobo (Simons & Fennig, 2018). In fact, different ISO codes were assigned for Binukid and Higaonon in Ethnologue, 'bkd' for Binukid and 'mba' for Higaonon. Supposedly, only one ISO code must be assigned to a language though it has several dialects. Another problem is that Higaonon is not even a dialect of Binukid. It is a name of a tribal group who speaks Binukid instead. This finding challenges the works of Elkins (1974) who classified Manobo as the mother language of Binukid, and that Binukid is spoken by the Higaonon people.

These inconsistencies, together with the fact that there is an insufficiency of lexicostatistical or genetic relationship studies on these three Binukid varieties, encouraged me, the present researcher, to confirm the genetic relationship of these varieties through the conduct of a contemporary lexicostatistical study using the Automated Similarity Judgement Program (ASJP).

Socio-Demographic Profile

Socio-demographic profile or simply demographic profile refers to the particular characteristics or attributes of a population (Salkind, 2010). This may include age, gender, monthly income, educational attainment, and other personal attributes that could potentially influence the data gathered and the findings of the study. In this study, socio-demographic profile only includes age, dialect spoken, other languages spoken, and highest educational attainment. These personal attributes are deemed to be important in this study since it would give me a background information as to the aptness of the chosen informants for the study.

This goes to say that the socio-demographic profile in this study serves as an inclusion criterion as well on who are to be considered as best fit informants for the study. When these personal attributes are not scrutinized, these would potentially affect the data gathered and eventually the findings of the study. Age is one personal attribute included in this study since it is believed to have an effect on the responses of the informants. The elderly for example are more mature as to how they express themselves. It is observed that the elderly have depth in their reflections compared to the younger ones. They are observed to have a profound knowledge and wisdom on a lot of things as they aged (Knauper et al., 2016).

Since this study, involves translation of vocabularies from one language into the native tongue of the informants, the elderly are considered fit to do this. It is believed that adults more specifically those whose age ranges from 60 years old and above could provide more accurate translations of words, from one language to their native tongue.

In most cases, the elderly use their native tongue often during communicative activities like speaking and writing compared to their young counterparts. They usually use their native language especially when talking to their children, grandchildren, and their peers. In fact, the study by Alwin and McCammon (2001) and Verhaeghen (2003) revealed that older adults tend to have larger vocabularies and greater lexical knowledge compared to younger adults (Rossi & Diaz, 2016). In addition, Juncos-Rabadan, Pereiro, and Rodriguez (2005) claimed that older adults tend to produce longer and more lexically diverse utterances. Based on this premise, I would assert that they are more knowledgeable in terms of translation of words from their second language to their native tongue thus making them best fit in this study.

In addition, the dialect spoken of the respondents is also an important factor to be considered in this study. Since this study involves translation of words from the second language to the native tongue of the informants, I must come up with an equal number of informants from each tribal group. This is to assure that each tribal group is well-represented to avoid possible biases.

Moreover, another factor to look into are the other dialects spoken by the informants. Learning a second language could potentially affect one's knowledge on his mother tongue. In some cases, people would find it difficult to translate vocabularies from their second language to their native tongue or vice versa. This is because their knowledge on the second language may override on their knowledge of their native tongue. This case has been observed in the studies conducted by Kaushanskaya, Yoo, and Marian (2011). Their study on English–Mandarin bilinguals implies that a person's experiences in the second language can affect his communicative performance in the native language, and that exposure to second language can either facilitate or reduce our linguistic competence in the native language.

The same findings were also reported by Marian and Spivey (2003) who stressed that knowledge of second language impacts the ability to manage information in the native language. This phenomenon when the second language learning affects the first language or vice versa is called crosslinguistic influence which was popularized by Weinrich in 1953 and further investigated by Lado in 1968 (Ilomaki, 2005; Magno, 2017).

Finally, the last indicator under the socio-demographic profile in this study is the highest educational attainment. I believed that it is relevant to look into the highest educational attainment of the informants since this could potentially affect as well to the accuracy of translations of the wordlist. Research shows that the more educated the person is, the more he becomes contaminated with his second language. In reverse, the less educated the person is, the lesser tendency that he becomes contaminated with his second language.

Language contamination in this context is better explained through the lens of the first-language attrition phenomenon. Language attrition in the words of Schmid (2008) is a process of loss, of forgetting, and of deterioration. Accordingly, speakers tend to forget some vocabularies in their first language as they learned a second language. For example, most Filipinos abroad would find it difficult to return speaking their mother tongue as they find it difficult to do so.

However, Levy, McVeigh, Marful, and Anderson (2007) in their study, claimed that forgetting our native language does not imply that we use it less, rather, this forgetfulness suggests that we actively inhibit our native language as it distracts us as we speak our second language. This forgetfulness may actually be an adaptive strategy to facilitate better learning in a second language. Whatever it might be–forgetfulness or inhibition, still, the level of education of the informants is considered as an important factor in this study as it potentially hampers vocabulary retention and retrieval in the first language.

Genetic Relationship of Languages and Language Divergence

Genetic (or genealogical) relationship among languages and language divergence are two interesting topics in applied linguistics. It goes to say that these two concepts are interesting avenues for linguistic research as well. Just like human beings, languages are genetically related with each other especially when these languages come from the same language family. For example, Spanish, French, and Italian came from their parent language Latin. One indicator that these languages are descendants of the same parent language is the similarity of their phonemes and morphemes (Posner & Cremona, 1963).

On the other hand, language divergence (also called 'time depth') refers to the separation of languages from their parent language. When languages separate from their parent language, new words arise while others are replaced. Moreover, sounds change, meanings evolve, grammar morphs, and speech communities diverged into dialects and then become distinct languages (Gray, Atkinson, & Greenhill, 2011).

Examining the genetic relationship among languages and language divergence is significant to understand language development. By tracing genetic relationships and divergence, one can build a phylogenetic classification which is of importance for linguists, historians, and anthropologists to understand language ancestry. By examining the genetic relationship among the Higaonon, Talaandig, and Bukidnon Binukid varieties, inconsistencies on the reports of these Binukid varieties would be solved.

The Higaonon, Talaandig, and Bukidnon Binukid Varieties

Bukidnon is a province of diverse ethnic communities. It is the home of the seven tribes who were believed to be the original settlers of the province. Three of these seven tribes are the Higaonon, Talaandig, and Bukidnon. These tribes are known to be speaking the Binukid language though inconsistencies on the reports regarding this language still exist at present, which I intend to address in this study.

Binukid is an ethnic language spoken in the north–central part of Mindanao particularly in Bukidnon. Binukid speech communities are also found in Misamis Oriental, Agusan del Norte, Agusan del Sur, and some parts of Cotabato. In terms of phylogeny, Binukid is considered to be part of the following subgroups of Austronesian, in descending order: Malayo-Polynesian; Greater Central Philippines; Manobo; and, North Manobo (Elkins, 1974; Peng & Billings, 2008).

One tribe known to be speaking Binukid are the Higaonon people. In terms of physique, Higaonons are of medium built with lighter skin complexion averaging about five feet and two inches in terms of height. Due to intermarriage between the natives and the Spanish colonizers, many Higaonons have prominent European features, curved nose, deep-set eyes and prominent cheeks. In this study, their language would be called Higaonon Binukid variety.

On the other hand, Talaandig is an ethnic group in the province of Bukidnon, found in the areas surrounding Mt. Kitanglad particularly in the towns of Talakag and Lantapan (Sumbalan, Mirasol, Mordeno, & Canoy, 2001). In the midst of advancement, modernization, and globalization, Talaandigs have preserved most of their beliefs, customs, practices, and traditions. In this study, their language would be called Talaandig Binukid variety. Meanwhile, it is interesting to note that Mt. Kitanglad is considered by both Talaandigs and Higaonons as their sacred "temple" and ancestral home.

Last among the three is the Bukidnon tribe whose ancestors are believed to be coming from the coastal places of Misamis Oriental and in some areas in north central Mindanao (Lynch & Clotet, 1967). Their means of living is through gathering foods and swine agriculture. In addition, embroidering garments and applique making are just two skills mastered by the women members of the tribe. The provincial website specified Bukidnon tribe as Binukid speakers which simply implies that the other ethnic groups in Bukidnon do not speak the same language. Meanwhile, in this study, the language spoken by the Bukidnon tribe would be called Bukidnon Binukid variety.

To avoid confusion, let me underscore some important terms. There are three terms that I would mostly use in this study in quiet similar ways. These are the *Bukidnon tribe*, *province of Bukidnon* or *Bukidnon province*, and *people or citizens of Bukidnon* or simply *Bukidnons*. *Bukidnon tribe* obviously refers to one of the seven ethnic groups who originally settled in the province of Bukidnon. One can be a '*Bukidnon*' by virtue of his residency in the province of Bukidnon but he may not necessarily be a member of the Bukidnon tribe.

Phonetic Variations and Sound Correspondences

Phonetic variation is one exciting phenomenon in sociolinguistics. Several researchers have been investigating on what influences phonetic variations and one primary finding among all these researches is because of dialect contact (Schmidt & Herrgen, 2011; Trudgil, 1986; Wang & Lien, 1993; William & Lien, 2014). Dialect contact or in a broader sense 'language contact' happens when two or more speakers from different linguistic backgrounds interact while unconsciously sharing their phonological competences with each other (Matras, 2009). Some common phenomena of language contact are language convergence and borrowing which resulted to code-mixing and code switching. As we interact with one another, we will be able to influence other's language and even adopt some of their linguistic nuances in terms of pronunciation, accent, and intonation. This eventually causes phonetic variations of languages even among dialects.

Some phonetic variations are evident in cases of phonemic free variation and allophonic free variation. Basically, free variation refers to an alternative pronunciation of a word (or of a phoneme in a word) that does not alter the word's meaning (Cruttenden, 2014; Nordquist, 2018; Radford, Atkinson, Britain, Clahsen, & Spencer, 2009; Yavas, 2006; Zsiga, 2012). For example, the lexical item 'either' can be both pronounced as /iðər/ or /aɪðər/. This is an example of phonemic free variation. Allophonic free variation is found on the example /damɪ/ and /ramɪ/, both are Filipino words which means 'many'. Phonetic variations also occur between full and reduced vowels in stressed and unstressed syllables like in the word 'affix' (Välimaa-Blum, 2005). When this word is used as verb, the first syllable adopts a schwa sound /ə/ as in /əˈfɪks/. On the other hand, when the word 'affix' is used as a noun, the first syllable adopts a more prominent vowel /æ/ as in /æˈfɪks/.

Meanwhile, languages that are known to be genetically related show recurrent sound correspondences or simply 'correspondences' in words with similar meanings. These words that contain similar sound correspondences and meanings are called 'cognates'. These cognates were formed as distinct vocabularies as these languages diverged or split from each other or from their parent language. For example, *'grazie'* in Italian and *'gracias'* in Spanish are cognates since these two languages are considered as Romance Languages, which are descendants of Latin. These two lexical items are similar since they share sound correspondences /g/, /r/, and /a/ which are indications of genetic relationship between languages. One good characteristic of sound correspondences in cognates is that they are preserved over time since sound changes take place in a regular basis.

In the comparative method of language reconstruction, examining correspondences is the main step. It this way, researchers will be able to establish relatedness of languages. However, determining correspondences in cognates takes a lot of time when done manually. And so, linguists who are interested in computational linguistics have designed computer programs in aid of language reconstruction. Examples of these programs are the Reconstruction Engine (RE) designed by Lowe and Mazaudon (1994) and the programs designed and proposed by Melamid (1999) and Koehn and Knight (2001).

Lexicostatistics, Glottochronology, and ASJP

Lexicostatistics was formulated by Morris Swadesh (a professor of anthropology and linguistics) in 1950s (Hymes, 1970). Basically, lexicostatistics as expressed simply by Hymes (1960) is a method to study genetic relationship of languages using the cognates from the core vocabularies proposed by Swadesh in 1950s. In other words, it is used to determine degrees of relationship between and among languages by examining the cognates of these languages and the sound correspondences of these cognates. It is a tool to estimate the degree of 'mutual intelligibility' between languages.

As explained by Nelson (2001), with the use of lexicostatistics, language researchers and linguists compare vocabularies of languages under study and determine the percentage of similarity of these languages to establish relationship. Moreover, with the use of lexicostatistical method one can create a language tree based on the percentage of shared cognates between and among the languages under study. Cognates are words in different languages that come from the same parent language. And so, languages that are closely related share a certain degree of similarity like in the case of Spanish and Italian.

Meanwhile, glottochronology is always associated with lexicostatistics since it deals in particular with phylogenetic relationship among languages (Jassem & Campbell, 2013). While lexicostatistics examines cognancy of vocabularies in Swadesh wordlist to elicit genealogical relationship of languages, glottochronology utilizes the frequency of this cognancy to determine language depth (or language divergence). Thus, glottochronology is somehow understood as an extension of lexicostatistics. Since, it holds the assumption on the constant rate of word retention or loss, this methodology is capable of determining language depth and eventually subgrouping of previously not known to be related languages. And so, lexicostatistics is a broader approach than glottochronology since one is required to know the cognancy of Swadesh's vocabularies through lexicostatistics before one would know language depth through glottochronology.

The accounts on basic assumptions of lexicostatistics are discussed in the works of Gudschinsky (1956) and Sankoff (1970). To encapsulate, these assumptions state: every language contain core vocabularies that are relatively less subject to lexical loss and change due to its semantic stability that is tested through time; and that the retention of these core vocabularies in these languages as time goes by indicate a genetic relationship of these languages.

Classical Methodology using Lexicostatistics

As mentioned previously, lexicostatistics is used to determine genetic relationship, time depth (language divergence), and subgrouping (Nelson,

2001). Traditionally, it requires a manual examination of cognates and stochastic computation on time depth and language divergence.

The following procedures were advanced by Gudschinsky (1956): First, *collecting of comparable word lists from the languages under study*. The collection of vocabularies from the languages under study using the Swadesh wordlist is the first step in doing lexicostatistics. The Swadesh wordlist must be translated in the target languages under study.

Second, *determining the probable cognates*. After the translated data have been collected, the next step is to analyze the words in the languages under study for probable cognates. True cognates are words in languages that descended from a common parent language. Since they come from a common parent language, these words share phonetic and semantic similarities making them conclusive evidence of genetic relationship. In other words, cognates are identified by matching the words of the languages under study by similarity of phonetic structure and meaning. Cognates can be detected when two phonemes are consistently found in the same relative position. For example, many words in L1 with initial consonant sound / t / have been found to be corresponding with words of the same meaning in L2 with initial sound / d /. The occurrence of these sound correspondences in many pairs of words under study are evidences of true cognates. And so, the more cognates found in the languages under study, the more they are genetically related like in the case of Spanish and Italian.

Third, *computing the time depth*. Time depth refers to the time (in years) that has elapsed as two languages split or diverged. It is done by converting the number of cognates into percentage by dividing the number of probable cognates by the total number of pairs of words compared. The formula to compute time depth is $t = log\ C\ 2\ log\ r$ where: t stands for the assumed time depth in millenia; C represents for the percent of cognates; and, r is "constant" (also called "index"), that is, the percent of cognates assumed to remain in the language as it diverged from a parent language as years go by. Meanwhile, *log* means 'logarithm of' while *log C* means the logarithm of the percent of probable cognates registered, and *2 log r* means twice the logarithm of the constant (Lees, 1953).

Fourth, *computing the range or margin of error*. In statistics, computing the margin of error is a way to set an amount of error that is tolerable. Since it is possible that examining pair of cognates from two languages by two separate researchers could yield two different results, it is necessary to come up with an estimate of its accuracy. Time depth is expressed according to range of years rather than specific number of years. Thus, in lexicostatistics, it is expressed in millennium or a thousand years.

Margin of error in lexicostatistics is computed based on the assumption that lexical changes in languages happen randomly thus producing a normal curve when plotted statistically. Usually, the margin of error is set to 5 percent (or lower) so that the level of confidence is approximately at 95 percent (or higher). In this case, the higher the level of confidence, the wider the range of years, and the higher the probability that the true answer lies within the range of years indicated. In other words, the narrower the range of years, the lesser the probability that the true answer is found within the range.

Fifth, *computing the dips (optional)*. Dips simply refers to the degrees of lexical relationship between languages under study. Since lexicostatistical techniques can only provide a tentative dating, it could mislead researchers and readers as to the specific years or months when two languages split or diverged from each other. For this reason, it is necessary to consider data in terms of dips rather than historical dates. With consideration of dips, lexical relationship of languages can be established objectively. Lexical relationship in dips can be computed using the formula, $d=14 \frac{\log C}{2 \log r}$. The result which is expressed in terms of time in millennia may then be multiplied by 14 or the time in years by 0.014 (Gudschinsky, 1955).

On the other hand, Heggarty (2010) and Zhang and Gong (2016) suggested the following steps:

First, using the 100 or 200 wordlist by Swadesh as glosses, conduct a word assembly from the languages under study. The wordlist by Swadesh has been used to gather linguistic data sets from different languages like the Indo-European and Austronesian languages (e.g., Lohr, 2000).

Second, determine lexical cognates by examining recurrent sound correspondences. These recurrent sound correspondences in cognates show a strong evidence that the languages under study come from a common origin. The word "recurrent" in this context means that sound correspondences must happen in at least two matching cases. Researches have shown that these recurrent sound correspondences are present in vocabularies of languages with phylogenetic relationships (Bergsland & Vogt, 1962; Hoijer, 1956). Other linguists like Nelson (2001) removed borrowed words manually from languages before doing a lexicostatistical comparison of languages, while others like in the works of SIL linguists modified the list to fit in to the setting where these words were used (Elkins, 1974).

In summary, the lexicostatistical working procedure includes the following (Geisler & List, 2009): first, use the Swadesh wordlist to conduct word assembly from the languages under study; second, make sure to translate this word assembly into the target languages under study; third, look for cognates by identifying recurring sound correspondences from the word assembly; fourth, quantify the identified cognates into percentage; and, fifth, establish the genetic relationship of languages under study by computing the dips and time depth using the given formula.

Related Studies Employing Classical Lexicostatistics

Below are several studies that made use of lexicostatistics as a methodology. These studies were conducted to illuminate language history by examining the genetic relationship and time–depth of these languages under study.

In the study of Miller (1984) on the case of two Uto–Aztecan studies a revised 100–item Swadesh wordlist were used in 36 Shoshone (or Numic) varieties. The findings revealed that 62 out of 100 items in the wordlist were found to be cognates in all 36 varieties. However, there were 11 items common to all except in one variety. Meanwhile, there were two lexical items common to all Uto-Aztecan languages; these were 'path' and 'tooth'. The finding implies that with the use of lexicostatistics, Uto-Aztecan languages are found to be closely related with each other. Lexicostatistics, therefore, is a potential linguistic tool to determine relationship among languages.

Moreover, another study explored the genealogical relationship among the Romance languages which included Daco-Rumanian, Latin, Italian, French, Portuguese, Spanish, and Catalan. Using the same techniques proposed by Miller (1984), the study revealed that there were 47 items out of 100 items by Swadesh were common to all of these languages. For some linguists and language researchers, this commonality of cognacy is not surprising since these Romance languages have been known to be fractions of their parent language, Latin. Hence, the findings strengthened the fact that these languages are genetically related with each other.

Other studies that made use of lexicostatistical methods are found in the works of Urreiztieta-Rivera (1980) on the Basque and Caucasian languages; Wimbish (1986) on the Zambales mountain languages in the Philippines; Shosted (2000) on Romani, Hindustani, and Czech languages; Harmon (2007) on Kagayanen and the Manobo languages in the Philippines; Starostin (2017) on Nubian, Nara, and Tama languages in Northeast Africa; Seid and Adigeh

(2017) on the Aari dialects in Ethiopia; and the latest by Ono (2019) on the Ainu dialects in Japan. In general, these studies were able to verify the genetic relationship of these languages.

In particular, Urreiztieta-Rivera (1980) claimed that Basque and Caucasian languages do not show high percentage of cognates. However, it appeared that there were evidences that implied that these languages are genetically related. Moreover, the researcher emphasized the inconclusiveness of the findings. Accordingly, further lexicostatistical studies must be done to validate previous findings on the relationship of these two languages. Meanwhile, Wimbish (1986) was able to validate that the Ayta (alternately called 'Negrito') languages in the mountains of Zambales, Philippines were genetically related. Thus, an Ayta Language phylogeny was created at the end of the study.

On the other hand, Shosted (2000), focused on Indo-European languages such as Romani, Hindustani, and Czech and was able to confirm the genetic affiliation of these languages. Moreover, Starostin (2017) validated three members of East Sudanic Language family–the Nubian, Nara, and Tama languages. The findings revealed that these three languages are genetically associated and that these East Sudanic languages were probably older than the Indo-European languages. Meanwhile, Seid and Adigeh (2017) did the same study on the Aari dialects in Ethiopia: Gayl, Sido, Woba, Layda, Biyo, Shengama, Baaka, Kure, and Kaysa. The findings revealed that Layda is the epicenter of these dialects since the other dialects shared much of their lexical items with Layda. On the other hand, the findings showed that Kaysa and Gayl are much different compared to the remaining seven Aari varieties.

In addition, Harmon (2007) was able to validate that Kagayanen, a Philippine language, is in fact part of the Manobo language family. However, the study revealed that Kagayanen shared many lexical innovations with the Bisayan languages than its Manobo language counterparts. In other words, Kagayanen speakers borrowed a number of Bisayan words which eventually became part of the Kagayanen language system. Meanwhile, the latest lexicostatistical study was done by Ono (2019) on the Ainu dialects in Japan and proved that these dialects were genetically related which posed a discrepancy to some previous lexicostatistical studies on these dialects.

One notable study that employed the classical methodology of lexicostatistics was conducted by Nelson (2001) among the three languages in Northern, Central, and Southern Luzon–the Tagalog, Bikolano, and

Ilokano. The researcher aimed to examine the historical relations among the three languages. Moreover, the researcher aimed to confirm his assumption that Ilokano and Tagalog share the most lexical similarities than Ilokano–Bikolano pair, and Bikolano–Tagalog pair. One unique procedure done by the researcher was the removal of loan words from other languages. This is to avoid the tendency of attaining skewed results in examining the relationship of these languages.

After identifying loan words, the researcher replaced the words with its synonym or the older form of the word in that particular language. If replacement could not be found, the word was automatically deleted from the wordlist. However, if the researcher noticed that the word is more influenced by other Philippine languages, the word will not be deleted from the wordlist. Hence, the original 100–wordlist was whittled down to 89 words. However, the researcher failed to mention how the identification of borrowed words was done. The next step that the researcher did was to perform a lexicostatistical comparison of the languages. Once completed, then the dates of divergence were determined through glottochronological comparisons.

Results showed that there was an equal degree of relationship between Tagalog and Ilokano, and Tagalog and Bikolano. In other words, the ratio of common core lexical items is the same for Tagalog and Ilokano as it is for Tagalog and Bikolano. The researcher's assumption that Tagalog and Ilokano are more genetically related is based on the fact that the areas where the Tagalog people settled are closer to the areas in the north where Ilokano speakers lived. Whereas, Bicolano speakers are settled in the south much farther to the Tagalog region. Hence, the finding of this study is surprising for the researcher. As to glottochronology using the formula $t = \log C / 2\log r$, this study revealed the following: Tagalog and llokano the same with Tagalog and Bikolano split about 2,200 years ago; and, Ilokano and Bikolano split about 4,000 years ago. This implies that Tagalog, llokano, and Bicolano descended from a common language family, while both Ilokano and Bikolano are equally related to Tagalog than to each other.

Linguists like Nelson (2001) acknowledged the fact that doing lexicostatistics and glottochronology in investigating genetic relationship of languages especially in those times is still premature and inconclusive. Much evidence is still needed to come up with a definitive conclusion on the genetic relationship and phylogenetic classifications of languages under study. However, the confirmation that Tagalog, Ilokano, and Bikolano languages are of common origin is justifiable. So, with the case of the Uto-Aztecan and Romance languages mentioned in the previous pages. Meanwhile, linguists and language researchers were never tired of studying and constructing advanced methodologies in doing lexicostatistics and glottochronology. Hence, the introduction of the contemporary methodology on lexicostatistics.

Contemporary Methodology on Lexicostatistics

It was Swadesh in 1950s who introduced the idea of wordlist from 200 to 100 lexical items considered to be the core vocabularies of any language which are assumed to be more resistant to language change. Some linguists suggested to use much smaller lexical items in the Swadesh wordlist. For example, Dolgopolsky (1986) suggested 15 items, Starostin (2000) proposed 35 items, Baxter and Ramer (2000) suggested 33 items, while Holman et al. (2008) recommended 40 items only out from the 100 or 200 Swadesh wordlists. On the contrary, other linguists and language researchers advocated using much bigger word assembly. For example, Greenberg (1993), Huang (1997), Jiang (2007), Li (1995), Newman (1995), and Ruhlen (1994) suggested to use 300–500 lexical items to attain more conclusive result. Meanwhile, Heggarty (2010) emphasized that linguistic experiences, exposure, and intuitions are the main considerations in the construction of these wordlists.

Moreover, there existed other quantitative approaches in comparative and historical language researches (e.g., Baxter & Ramer, 2000; Kessler, 2001; Lohr, 2000; Oswalt, 1971; Ringe, 1992;). Still, with the use of wordlist, genetic relationship and phylogenetic classifications among languages can be verified by determining recurrent sound correspondences among cognates.

Furthermore, in the advent of computer technology and computational linguistics, another way of determining genetic relationship and time depth of languages was born. Through algorithm and complex computer programming, one can now easily examine genealogical relationship, time depth, and subgrouping of languages. One known program that was designed to measure language relationships, time depth, and subgrouping is the ASJP (Automated Similarity Judgement Program)

Doing Lexicostatistics using ASJP

Automated Similarity Judgement Program (ASJP) was developed by a group of IT experts, anthropologists, and linguists collectively called 'ASJP

Consortium". ASJP is a computer program designed to analyze genetic relationship and time depth or language divergence using algorithms and complex computer commands (Wichmann et al., 2010). In other words, it is an automated alternative tool in doing lexicostatistical studies. There are four major advantages of ASJP: first, since it is automated, it is more objective than the classical lexicostatistical methods; second, it uses a uniform analytical approach across languages in the world assembled in one database; third, does not rely on cognate percentages but on lexical similarity determined using Levenshtein distances; and fourth, it uses of a formula to calculate dates of language divergence.

Levenshtein Distance is an algorithm invented by Vladimir Levenshtein in 1965. It is basically a number that indicates whether two strings are more similar or more different. When used in lexicostatistical studies, these strings could be represented by words. The higher the Levenshtein Distance between two words being compared, the more they are different. An elaborate discussion on Levenshtein Distance is found on the works on Serva and Petroni (2008).

The ASJP consortium aimed to develop an automatic method to determine relationship of languages and eventually reconstruct groupings and subgroupings of these languages. This reconstruction may refine and enrich existing phylogenetic relationship of languages that are plotted in language trees. In other words, it may correct inconsistencies in phylogenies while giving identities to languages that are yet unclassified. Moreover, it may help linguists and language researchers to distinguish cognates and loan words. Finally, it may validate or invalidate findings of classical lexicostatistical studies. All of these features are embedded in the ASJP by the consortium to come up with a more objective method in determining relationship among languages.

In ASJP, the reconstruction process is based on the distances between languages, dialects, and protolanguages plotted on a matrix. These distances were originally based on the number of cognates found on pairs of languages. Later experiments by Holman et al. (2008) elucidated that adding typological data can make lexicostatistical method more accurate. This typological data is sourced out from the database used for the World Atlas of Language Structures (WALS) (Comrie, 2005), to which many ASJP members contributed much. This typological data is composed of structural properties which include the lexical, phonological, and grammatical attributes of languages. Adding these structural properties strengthen the lexicostatistical methods in determining relationship of languages.

Related Lexicostatistical Studies that Employ ASJP

The study conducted by Wichmann and Rama (2018) compared the performance of the Automated Similarity Judgment Program (ASJP) method of classification across the world's language families and the qualitative studies on the relationship of these languages done by the experts. It turned out that ASJP yielded a relatively poor performance especially in the Austronesian languages. This poor performance is attributed to the mismatching reports of experts and the result of ASJP classification. These inaccuracies contributed to the amount of error in the classification of Austronesian languages. And so, the members of the ASJP consortium have taken necessary investigations as to consolidate the reports of the Austronesian languages from experts and the result of the ASJP classification. Hence, this opens for more research opportunities to linguists and language researchers on the Austronesian languages.

Moreover, a study conducted by Jäger and Wichmann (2016) aimed at constructing a phylogenetic tree on the languages across all continents. The primary method they used is phonetic transcription only. Meaning, they did not rely on cognate judgement from experts. Finally, the language tree that they were able to construct from the world languages across continents recaptured the already established language classifications.

This study was conceived to explore on the inconsistency on the reports and records of the Binukid language, an ethnic language of the native inhabitants of the province of Bukidnon. The province pride itself as the home of seven tribes namely Manobo, Matigsalug, Tigwahanon, Umayamnon, Higaonon, Talaandig, and Bukidnon. From the foundation of the province in 1917 until now, these seven tribes gather altogether sometime between February and March for the "Kaamulan Festival". Kaamulan is from the Binukid term 'amul' which means 'to gather'.

All throughout these years, it has become a common knowledge in the province that these seven tribes speak the same language–Binukid. However, inconsistencies on the reports and records of the Binukid language still existed. For example, the Presidential Assistant for National Minorities (PANAMIN) which is now defunct, and Industan (2009), an academician and a native Bukidnon classified the Binukid language into three varieties spoken by the Higaonon, Talaandig, and the Bukidnon tribes. However, the other four Binukid varieties were never mentioned.

Another inconsistent report came from the glottochronological works of Elkins (1974). Accordingly, Binukid is spoken by the Higaonon and Talaandig tribes. The Bukidnon tribe were never mentioned as a Binukid–speaking group. In addition, the reports of Elkins (1974) rejected the common belief that the other remaining ethnic groups are Binukid speakers as well. Adding to the inconsistency is the statement form the official website of Bukidnon provincial government. The website claimed that Binukid is a dialect of the Bukidnon tribe. The website as of this writing does not even mentioned that Binukid is also spoken by the Higaonon, Talaandig, and the four other tribes.

Moreover, the inconsistency expands as Ethnologue, a project by SIL International, reported that Binukid is a sister language of Higaonon, Kagayanen, and Manobo (Simons & Fennig, 2018). The fact that SIL International, through Ethnologue, assigned different ISO codes for Binukid (bkd) and Higaonon (mba) proved that SIL International considered these two as separate langauges. The problem is that Higaonon is not even a language, it is one of the ethnic groups who speak the Binukid language. Besides, this report challenges the Proto-Manobo Theory of Elkins (1974) which stressed that Manobo is the mother language of Binukid.

These inconsistencies motivated me to examine the genetic relationship of the Binukid language varieties particularly the varieties spoken by the Higaonon, Talaandig, and Bukidnon ethnic groups. Likewise, my motivation to pursue this study was strengthened with the fact that there are no lexicostatistical studies as of yet that focus on the Binukid language varities. Since there were methodological issues on the classical lexicostatistics, I opted to employ the Automated Similarity Judgement Program (ASJP), a contemporary method in determining genetic relationships and time depth. I asked assistance from the ASJP consortium, the developer of the ASJP for the automated analysis of my data. I also sought help from an expert in the University of Southern Mindanao especially for the analysis of phonetic variations and similarities of my data.

CHAPTER 3
METHODOLOGY

Presented in this chapter are the research design, role of the researcher, research materials, data collection, data analysis, trustworthiness, and ethical consideration.

Research Design

Due to the nature of the study and the absence of 'constructs' or 'variables' to be examined in terms of their relationship using specific statistical tools, this study employed a case study approach. Creswell and Creswell (2017) treats a case study research as a qualitative approach while Stake (1994) stressed that case study is an approach which can be treated qualitatively and quantitatively. Authors may disagree on whether a case study must be treated qualitatively or both while others disagree whether it must be treated as an approach or methodology. Despite the disagreement, the common agreement is that in a case study, the researcher analyzes a case or cases for a period of time through a deliberate and in-depth collection of data sourced out from multiple sources from reports, audiovisual materials, and documents or through an interview and observation. The researcher describes the case or cases and come up with themes.

In this study, the case studied is the inconsistency of the reports of Elkins (1974), PANAMIN, Summer Institute of Linguistics (SIL), and the Bukidnon provincial website on the language of these tribes (Higaonon, Talaandig, Bukidnon) and the Binukid language classification. I believe that when genetic relationship is examined among the Binukid varieties spoken by these tribes, its language classification and time depth will be clarified and its phylogenetic subgrouping will be constructed or reconstructed.

Specifically, this study employed the *instrumental case study approach* by Stake (1994) which further describes, explores, explain, and illustrate an existing case. In this study, I intended to explore on the inconsistency of the language identities and classifications of the Binukid language varieties.

Role of the Researcher

In the words of Creswell and Creswell (2017), the role of the researcher in a qualitative research is critical since he collects the data himself and analyze it thoroughly. My role as the present researcher is that of an observer (etic)–from an outside view, therefore, more objective. I collected data objectively, coded it, and have them analyzed by Holman, et al., through the use of Automated Similarity Judgment Program (ASJP). I took time to jot down my biases, thoughts, feelings, and premature analysis on the data gathered.

In addition, as Postholm and Skrovset (2013) stated it, qualitative researchers have multi-faceted roles that will challenge them cognitively and emotionally. So, I, as the researcher played as the main instrument in this research being the data gatherer, data recorder, data coder, and data interpreter. As the data gatherer, I personally gathered the data of my study from my informants from three barangays representing the three Binukid varieties.

As the data recorder, I gave my informants the luxury of time to translate the Swadesh 100 wordlist from Cebuano to Binukid. After that, I requested them to pronounce each word in the Binukid language while I was recording using an audio recorder in my cellphone. Moreover, as a data coder, I coded my data using the International Phonetic Alphabet and later on using the ASJP codes. After the coding process, I sent the data to my analysts, one from the University of Southern Mindanao and one from the University of California. As soon as I received the result, I interpreted and discussed it.

Research Participants

The study was conducted in the province of Bukidnon particularly in the municipalities of Sumilao, where most Higaonon people settled, Lantapan where most Talaandigs were located and in Casisang, Malaybalay City where the Bukidnon tribal groups lived. Sumilao is a 4th class municipality while Lantapan is a 1st class municipality of Bukidnon. Meanwhile, Casisang is a barangay of Malaybalay City, the capital of Bukidnon.

Purposeful or criterion–based sampling was used to determine the participants of the study. Six participants from each tribal group answered the instrument. These informants must be 60 years old and above. The age criterion is based on the assumption that elderly people are less contaminated with new vocabularies and are more resistant to language change. And so, they can provide a more accurate answer. Preferably, participants are literate with minimum educational attainment so they could write their answers themselves on the instrument. Three informants initially answered the questionnaire. After that, I triangulated their answers with the remaining three informants through a focus group discussion.

Research Materials

The research instrument used in this study was the 100–word Swadesh list. This list is composed of 100 core vocabularies that are considered by Swadesh (1955) as universal to all languages and are resistant to language change.

Swadesh was a linguist and a professor of linguistics and anthropology. It was in 1950s that he formulated the foundations of modern lexicostatistics and glottochronology after he was discharged from the school he was teaching for his political activities. His wordlist was initially composed of 200 basic and core vocabularies. These 200 words are assumed by Swadesh to be much less subject to change. These include pronouns, quantity, adjective, human noun, animal, environment, animal product, body part, body verb, perception verb, impact, motion, transfer, color, and time (Bowern, 2015).

In 1955, Swadesh published his final 100-wordlist. He stated that this wordlist contained more stable lexical items that are less prone to borrowing (Tadmor, Haspelmath, & Taylor, 2010; Zhang & Gong, 2016). This assumption was strengthened after the statistical comparison between the 200–wordlist and the 100–wordlist revealed that these two wordlists are both reliable, and that the Swadesh 100–wordlist is no different to the 200–wordlist (Zhang & Gong, 2016).

However, Holman et al. (2008) proposed a 40–wordlist comprising the most stable items of the 100–item wordlist based on their research. However, this study used the 100–wordlist as suggested by Holman himself in his email to me.

Data Collection

Before the conduct of the study, I submitted my paper first to the University of Mindanao Ethics Review Committee (UMERC) for ethical evaluation. As soon as I received the Certificate of Compliance from the committee, I immediately sent a communication letter (approved by the UM Research

Office) to the barangay captains or the gatekeepers of the three municipalities where I intended to conduct my study. After the schedule of conduct was set, I immediately coordinated with the barangay captain and the gatekeepers for the actual conduct of the study.

During the actual conduct of the study, three informants from each tribe were asked to translate the Swadesh wordlist into the Binukid language. After translating the wordlist, the informants were asked to read the wordlist for me to get the phonetic features of the given words like the sounds and stress. The reading activity were recorded using an audio recorder. Meanwhile, the other three informants were asked to participate for the focus group discussion. This was done to verify and triangulate the translation and pronunciation of the first three informants on the Swadesh wordlist.

In terms of duration, I allotted five months to finish this study. Duration simply refers to the amount of time spent in the conduct of the study from the conceptualization stage, data gathering, data analysis and interpretation, up to the writing of the research report. It must be noted that this study was successfully proposed and defended during the outline defense last October 2018, the last month of the first semester of the school year 2018–2019. After the outline defense, I allotted one and a half month for the University of Mindanao Ethics Review Committee (UMERC) to evaluate my study in terms of its ethical merit, that is from November until the second week of December 2018. After I was given the Certificate of Compliance on the third week of December, I immediately gathered data on the fourth week of the same month.

On the first week of January 2019, I coded my data using the ASJP codes and submitted it to Holman immediately for analysis. The second week of January was allotted for data interpretation and discussion of results which was written in Chapter 4 and 5 of this paper. Public forum immediately followed on the third week of March. Further, I allotted the third week of June for the final defense and the remaining three months for quality control. Hopefully, I will finish this study in October 2019.

Meanwhile, case studies usually employ multiple methods in collecting data depending on the nature of the case and the issues under study. However, in this study, the methods involved in the collection of data include: translation of the Swadesh 100-wordlist in the Higaonon, Talaandig, and Bukidnon Binukid varieties. It was done through oral interview or paper–and–pen approach; next step was the sound transcription using the International Phonetic Alphabet (IPA); the third step was another phonetic coding using the ASJP codes; and, the last step included computation and analysis of the codes using the Automated Similarity Judgment Approach (ASJP) by Eric W. Holman.

Data Analysis

The data analysis started during the transcription of the data gathered. As mentioned earlier, the translation and pronunciation of the wordlist were recorded on paper and on audio recorder. While listening to the recorded pronunciation, I noted the sounds involved and transcribed each word using the International Phonetic Alphabet (IPA) sound symbols. After the data were transcribed, I sent it to my analyst from the University of Southern Mindanao. As soon as I received the data, I immediately started interpreting it by examining the phonetic variations and phonetic similarities of the lexical items.

Meanwhile, I coded the data that I sent to my first analyst using a specialized set of ASJP codes provided by Eric W. Holman. I sent the data to Holman himself for the analysis on the genetic relationship of the Higaonon, Talaandig, and Bukidnon Binukid varieties. This is to substantiate and validate my interpretation of the data. ASJP makes use of logarithms and rigid computer programming to examine the genetic relationship of the languages under study, its time depth, and phylogenetic classification.

Trustworthiness

The current study adopted Lincoln and Guba (1986) trustworthiness criteria of qualitative studies. There are four criteria proposed by Guba (1981) to achieve a trustworthy study. These are credibility, transferability, dependability, and confirmability.

Credibility deals on the congruency of the findings of the study and the reality'. One criterion that establishes the credibility of the study is the researcher himself. In the words of Patton (1999), the researcher's credibility is extremely important since he is the main instrument in the collection and analysis of data.

Another criterion that establishes credibility of the study is the appropriateness of methods used. Since this study, is a study of a case, say the inconsistency of reports of the Binukid varieties relationship and subgrouping, instrumental case study approach is most suitable for it since it aims to describe, explore, explain, and illustrate a questionable case.

Further, triangulation is another factor that establishes credibility. In the present study, the researcher employed triangulation. In the words of Thurmond (2001), it is important to triangulate data to strengthen and enriched the thoroughness of the data collected thereby attaining more accuracy in the interpretation of data. Triangulation addresses the issue of deficiency of strategies in data collection. Moreover, informants were not forced to participate in the study. Only those who were genuinely willing and interested were involved in the study so the findings will not be compromised.

Meanwhile, informants could withdraw their participation anytime during the conduct of the study if they wish to. If given an ample time, the researcher will inform the informants on the findings of the study. Further, the researcher will have this paper reviewed by experts in the field of linguistics to make it more credible.

The next construct to be established to achieve trustworthiness of the study is the *transferability*. Tobin and Begley (2004) and Bitsch (2005) so with Anney (2014) stressed that transferability refers to the applicability of research findings to other situations. The findings of this study might be unique and might also become a basis to explore the genetic relationship, time depth, and sub-grouping of the languages of the remaining four other tribes.

Meanwhile, *dependability* in research refers to the consistency of results obtained if the research work is repeated over and over using the same methods with the same informants in the same context. I, as the present researcher believe that dependability was established in this study since the data of this study was analyzed through a rigorous algorithm of the software Automated Similarity Judgment Program (ASJP). Lincoln and Guba (1986) however stressed the close ties between credibility and dependability through an overlapping method of focus group and individual interview which I did during the data gathering. Moreover, the study was written thoroughly to enable the future researchers repeat this research work and most likely come up with the same results.

Lastly, *confirmability* is associated with objectivity in scientific research that makes use of instruments (Patton, 1990). However, Patton (1990) also recognized the fact that it is difficult to ensure real objectivity in research since even instruments are developed by humans and research informants are already contaminated with biases before they answer the research instruments.

To reiterate, triangulation was done in the conduct of the study to achieve confirmability. Aside from that, I invited experts in applied linguistics in the local, national, and international level (including Eric W. Holman) to review and evaluate my paper after I incorporated all the corrections and suggestions during the final defense. After all the corrections and feedbacks are given, I will gladly work on it to come up with a quality paper.

Ethical Consideration

The most important principles related to ethical considerations in research which will also be observed in this study are based on Bell and Bryman (2007).

Before the conduct of the study, I ensured that informants were properly informed about the objectives of the study. I explained to them that participation in this study is purely voluntary. That in case in the middle of the conduct of the study, they would refuse to continue answering the questionnaire, they will not be forced to do so. Full consent was obtained from the informants prior to their participation of the study.

The conduct of research tends to be risky at times to the participants and to the researcher as well. As defined by the University of California, Irvine Office of Research, risk is the potential injury or harm caused by the participation in a research study. Risk is multifaceted as it could be physical, legal, psychological, social, or economic (Shaw & Barrett, 2006).

Physical Risk, as stated by the Research Compliance Services of the University of Oregon, may include physical harm like pain, discomfort, injury, or disease brought forth by the research procedures and methods. This study however did not involve physical risk since this study did not employ physical stimuli that could potentially harm the participants. The participants of this study were not exposed to any sort of harmful chemicals, dangerous equipment, and risky procedures during the data gathering. Moreover, to ensure safety, the participants answered the questionnaires and underwent focus group discussion at the comfort of their own locality and home.

Psychological risks refer to the negative changes in the cognitive and affective processes of the participants due to their involvement in the research. Emotions like loss of self-esteem, anxiety, guilt, shock, confusion, embarrassment, and depression are psychological risks when these affective states were created after informants participated in research. Psychological risk also occurs when participants are deprived of sleep, hypnotized, or mentally stressed. Staging of fake assaults and emergency situations could also generate psychological risks since it can stress out participants. Sensitive topics like involvement in crime, sexual abuse, violence, and sexual preference could mentally stress out participants so it involves psychological risks. Though there are psychological risks that can potentially cause serious harm, however most psychological risks are minimal or transitory.

In this study however, participants were not asked about anything other than the translation of the given set of gloss in the questionnaire. After which, another group of respondents validated the translations. Since sensitive topics mentioned above were not the focus of this research endeavor so I did not talk about it with them.

Further, this study does not involve *social risks* since it does not engage participants to any form of embarrassment or alterations in their relationships. I, the researcher, assured to uphold privacy of personal information and confidentiality of data since assault to privacy and breaches of confidentiality may lead to embarrassment on the part of the respondents. It must be noted that participants were only asked to translate the gloss in the questionnaire and another group of participants validated it through a focus group discussion.

Meanwhile, this study does not also involve *economic risks*. In other words, it did not require financial costs on the part of the participants. All expenses necessary in the conduct of the study such as travel expense, data analyst fee, validator's fee, and the like were shouldered solely by me, the researcher. I did not ask even a single centavo from the participants in the conduct of this research.

In addition, this study does not implicate *legal risk (legal harm)*. Basically, legal risk refers to the possibility of causing an interaction between the participants and the court system. Or, when the participants will be held liable for a violation of the law due to their participation in the study. Legal risk also exists when a study examines sexual abuse, drug use, or criminal activity of the participants. However, since I only asked the participants to translate a set of gloss in the questionnaire and have it triangulated through a focus group discussion, it does not implicate legal risk or harm in anyway. Thus, respect for human dignity was upheld during the conduct of the study. In summary, no informants were harmed in anyway. No informants were threatened for any cause.

Though this study does not implicate significant risks, I assured to minimize risks that would possibly occur during the conduct of the study. Moreover, I submitted my paper to the University of Mindanao Ethics Review Committee (UMERC) to examine my research plan, research design, and methodology to determine inherent flaws that would possibly place participants at unnecessary risks. I ensured that participants' autonomy was maximized, possible risks were minimized, and benefits were maximized.

Benefits from social research maybe difficult to define. The closer definition of it is that "benefits are valued outcomes." At the personal level, finishing this research also entails finishing my doctorate degree in applied linguistics, but more than that, this study would utilize my knowledge in language research as a practicing linguist. At the academic level, this research endeavor would fill in the existing gap and inconsistencies on the report of the Binukid language varieties. The provincial government of Bukidnon and the academic community in the province would then be clarified as to whether real relationship exists among the three Binukid language varieties. Moreover, this research endeavor would somehow make the participants feel important as they are able to contribute to the study of their own language. Participants may feel the sense of 'pride' and 'identity' on their heritage.

Confidentiality of personal information about the informants was upheld as well. In the discussion of the result, informants were assigned with pseudonyms in case there was a necessity to single out informants. Confidentiality during the triangulation (focus group discussion) was strictly observed as well. I reminded the participants that they were prohibited to share personal and sensitive information to others who were not present during the triangulation (focus group discussion).

Furthermore, I ensured that *falsification* and *fabrication* of data was prohibited as well to ensure honesty and transparency. Falsification and fabrication were considered as two "cardinal sins" in research aside from plagiarism. When researcher manipulates research materials, data, findings, sample, including equipment used in the conduct of research, falsification is committed (Zietman, 2013).

To avert falsification and fabrication of data, I never changed, omitted, nor manipulated data from the participants. Further, I did not make up data just for the purpose of completing possible lacking data. In addition, I invited the gatekeepers to become the "overseers" of my data gathering procedures. I asked them to observe how I would retrieve the responses of the participants. I even asked one member of the University of Mindanao Ethics Review Committee (UMERC) to re-contact my participants for the purpose of validating whether I committed falsification and fabrication of data.

In addition, I ensured that all my discussions in this study were originally written by me, and that literature from other authors are properly paraphrased. And so, after I finished this written report, I will submit it to the university ethics committee again for plagiarism check through *Turnitin* to ensure that this paper is original and free from plagiarism.

Conflict of Interest (*COI*) in research refers to anything that can cause a divided loyalty between and among the researcher, the participants, and the institutions involved in the study. It may also refer to circumstances when a researcher manipulated the direction of his research in favor of his research sponsor or his personal desire to advance professionally (Braff, 2010).

COIs can occur in domains like financial (sponsorship, funding, financial interest in research outcomes); emotional (power imbalances in which participants feel coerced into participating); personal (personal gain from the research outcomes); and professional (undertaking research in your own organization with your own clients) (O'Brien, 2008).

This research endeavor however, was not in any way, sponsored or funded by any funding agencies. In addition, I did not coerce participants to participate in the study since participation in this study is fully voluntary. That in case they would refuse to become a participant, they will not be forced to become one. That in case they will decide to discontinue answering the questionnaire, they will be given the freedom to do it without threatening and harming them in any way possible. That after this research endeavor, I, the researcher will not gain any favor (for example, finances) from whoever since it is not sponsored or funded by any agency. That after this research endeavor, I, the researcher will only gain knowledge which can be used in the provincial government and academic community for free. And that, this research endeavor will not be conducted in my own organization but in localities where the qualified participants live. Thus, I would say, that there is no conflict of interest in this study.

Deception or *deceit* in research happens when researchers purposefully mislead participants by providing them with overt misdirection or false information about the research being conducted, whether it is in the procedures or the purpose of research itself (Miller, Wendler, & Swartzman, 2005). Incomplete disclosure is similar to deception or deceit. When a researcher withholds information about some aspect of the research, incomplete disclosure occurs.

In this study, deception (deceit) and incomplete disclosure was committed since I totally disclosed my objectives in the conduct of my study to the participants. In fact, the objectives of this study were written on the communication letter which was attached to the questionnaire for the participants to know. So, before they would answer the questionnaire, I woud read to them the letter and the objectives of the study to reiterate my purpose of conducting the study. The same process that did for the participants assigned in the focus group discussion. If given an ample time, I will inform the participants about the result of the study. In addition, my curriculum vitae is provided in the appendix for the perusal of the barangay officials, gatekeepers, and participants of the study. This is to give them vital contact information if ever they will have questions and complaints regarding the conduct of the study.

The last ethical concern which this study addresses is on *authorship*. The International Committee of Medical Journal Editors (ICMJE) (2017) states that authorship confers credit to whoever conducted and wrote the report of the research. There are four criteria proposed by ICMJE in which authorship should be based: the authors must have contributed substantially to the conception or design of the research, analysis, or interpretation of data of research; the authors must have drafted the research work or revised it critically for its intellectual content; the authors must be responsible for the final approval of the version to be published; and, must agree to be accountable for all aspects of the research work.

CHAPTER 4
RESULTS

Presented in this chapter are the results of the study conducted. It is in this chapter that I present the data gathered in tabular form which I enriched with description and explanation. The presentation of data and its description and explanation is organized according to the sequence of the research questions.

The Socio-Demographic Profile of the Informants

Shown in Table 1 is the distribution of informants in terms of age, dialect spoken, other languages spoken, and highest educational attainment. The table further presents that most informants particularly twelve of them are 60–65 years old comprising 66.7 percent of the total population. Moreover, three informants were 66–70 years old comprising 16.7 percent of the population. Meanwhile, two informants comprising 11.1 percent were 76–80 years old and one informant which only comprises 5.6 percent belonged to the 71–75 years old age bracket.

In terms of dialect spoken, I see to it that each tribe is well represented to come up with an equal number of informants from each tribe. As seen on the table below, I tapped six informants from the Higaonon, six from the Talaandig, and another six from the Bukidnon tribe each composing 33.3 percent of the total population. It must be noted that out of six, three respondents answered the instrument and the other three were formed as a focus group for the discussion and triangulation of the data gathered from the first three. This process was done throughout the entire data collection activity.

Table 1: *The Socio-Demographic Profile of the Informants*

Demographic Profile	Frequency	Percentage
Age		
60–65 years old	12	66.7
66–70 years old	3	16.7
71–75 years old	1	5.6
76–80 years old	2	11.1
Total	**18**	**100**
Dialect Spoken		
Binukid–Higaonon	6	33.3
Binukid–Talaandig	6	33.3
Binukid–Bukidnon	6	33.3
Total	**18**	**100**
Other Languages Spoken		
Cebuano	18	60
English	7	23.3
Filipino	5	16.7
Total	**30**	**100**
Highest Educational Attainment		
Elementary Level	7	38.9
Elementary Graduate	3	16.7
High School Level	1	5.6
High School Graduate	3	16.7
College Level	2	11.1
College Graduate	2	11.1
Total	**18**	**100**

The distribution of informants in terms of other languages spoken is also shown in the table. The table further shows that Cebuano is the other language mostly spoken by 18 informants (60 percent). Other languages spoken are English and Filipino, with seven (23.3percent) and five (16.7 percent) informants speaking it respectively.

Lastly, in terms of highest educational attainment, it can be gleaned from the table that seven informants (38.9 percent) reached elementary level, three informants (16.7 percent) graduated in elementary and another three (16.7 percent) graduated in high school. Meanwhile, two informants (11.1 percent) reached college level, another two (11.1 percent) graduated in college, and one informant (5.6 percent) reached high school level.

The Genetic Relationship of the Three Binukid Language Varieties

In this study, the genetic relationship of the three Binukid language varieties was examined through phonological variations and correspondences the use of the Automated Similarity Judgment Program (ASJP) software. Examination of phonological variations correspondences is one criterion to determine genetic relationship of languages. To come up with a more objective result, this method is further strengthened through the use of the Automated Similarity Judgment Program (ASJP) software.

Table 2.1: *Phonological Variation and Correspondences of Higaonon, Talaandig, and Bukidnon Binukid*

English Glosses	**Higaonon**	**Talaandig**	**Bukidnon**
Not	/hariʔ/, /hurʔa/	/hadiʔ/, /hudaʔ/	/hariʔ/
Many	/madakəl/	/madakəl/	/dakəl/
Two	/daruwa/	/daduwa/	/daruwa/
Long	/malayat/	/malaŋkaw/	/mataŋkaw/
Round	/liruŋ/, /liruŋliruŋ/	/lidənlidən/	/liruŋliruŋ/
Dry	/mamara/	/gaŋu/, /mamada/	/mamara/
Name	/ŋaran/	/ŋaran/, /ŋadan/	/ŋaran/
Dog	/asu/, /tiyalus/	/asɔ/	/asu/

Louse	/lusaʔ/	/lusaʔ/	/lisaʔ/
Root	/gamut/	/dalid/	/gamut/
Sun	/anlaw/	/anlaw/	/aldaw/
Rain	/uran/	/udan/	/uran/
Earth	/kalibutan/	/kalibutan/	/bugtaʔ/
Cloud	/gabunan/	/gabun/	/gabun/
Smoke	/ubəl/	/ubul/	/ubul/
Ash	/anuk/, /abu/	/anək/	/abu/
Ear	/taliNa/	/taliNa/, /taNila/	/taliNa/
Nose	/iruN/	/idəN/	/iduN/
Tooth	/Nipun/	/Nipən/	/Nipun/
Belly	/gətək/	/gətuk/	/gətuk/
Drink	/inum/	/inəm/	/inum/
Sleep	/tiruga/	/tiduga/	/tiruga/
Say	/kagi/, /ikagi/	/ikagi/, /ikagihi/	/ikagi/
Kill	/himatayan/	/himatayan/, /himatayi/	/himatayi/
Come	/dumini/, /dali/	/dini/	/dini/
Lie	/biruʔ/	/biduʔ/	/biduʔ/
Sit	/panuʔu/	/pinuʔu/	/pinuʔu/
Give	/ila/	/ila/, /ilahi/	/iʔila/
Black	/maitum/	/maitəm/	/maitum/
Night	/daləman/	/daləman/	/daluman/

The table below presents the phonological variations and correspondences of Higaonon, Talaandig, and Bukidnon Binukid. The first column consists of English glosses from the Swadesh 100-wordlist which vary when translated into the three Binukid varieties.

These variations are found in the second, third and fourth columns. It must be noted in the following discussions that the orthography of the varieties is immediately followed by its transcription. Meanwhile, the transcription symbols used are that of the International Phonetic Alphabet (IPA).

The first lexical item on the table is 'not' which can be translated into 'hari' /hariʔ/ or '*hura*' /hurʔa/ in Higaonon, '*hadi*' /hadiʔ/ or '*huda*' /hudaʔ/ in Talaandig and '*hari*' /hariʔ/ in Bukidnon. It is notable that similarities of phonemes occur in Higaonon /hariʔ/ or /hurʔa/ and the Bukidnon /hariʔ/. However, Talaandig preferred to use /hadiʔ/ or /hudaʔ/. In other words, Talaandig Binukid adopts the phoneme /d/ as in /hadiʔ/ or /hudaʔ/ while Higaonon and Bukidnon adopt the phoneme /r/ as in /hariʔ/ or /hurʔa/. All three cognates are phonetically similar with the exemption of the phonemes /r/ and /d/. This phenomenon is called allophonic free variation.

The second lexical item on the table is 'many' which can be translated as '*madakel*' /madakəl/ in both Higaonon and Talaandig and alternately '*dakel*' /dakəl/ in Bukidnon. This linguistic phenomenon when the unstressed syllable like '*ma*' in '*madakel*' is omitted can be associated with a phonological process known as "weak syllable deletion." Like in the first lexical entry, all phonemes of the three cognates are the same except that the prefix '*ma*' is omitted in the Bukidnon cognate.

The third lexical item is 'two' which can be translated as '*daruwa*' /daruwa/ in both Higaonon and Bukidnon and alternately '*daduwa*' /daduwa/ in Talaandig. Again, all phonemes of the three cognates are the same except that Higaonon and Bukidnon preferred the phoneme /r/ while Talaandig preferred /d/. It must be noted that this case also happened in the first lexical item. This is another case of allophonic free variation.

The fourth lexical item is 'long' which can be translated as '*malayat*' /malayat/ in Higaonon, '*malangkaw*' /malaŋkaw/ in Talaandig, and '*matangkaw*' /mataŋkaw/ in Bukidnon. In this case, all phonemes of the cognates from Talaandig and Bukidnon varieties are the same except that Talaandig adopts /l/ while Bukidnon preferred /t/. Meanwhile, /malayat/ is preferred to be used by Higaonon. Allophonic free variation also occurred in these lexical items

The fifth lexical item is 'round' which is equivalent to '*lirung*' /liruŋ/ or '*lirunglirung*' /liruŋliruŋ/ in Higaonon, '*lidenglideng*' /lidəŋlidəŋ/ in Talaandig, and '*lirunglirung*' /liruŋliruŋ/ in Bukidnon. It can be noticed that /liruŋliruŋ/ is both used by Higaonon and Bukidnon while Talaandig preferred /lidəŋlidəŋ/. Again, similarities of phonemes occur between Higaonon and

Bukidnon cognates except that /r/ is used by both Higaonon and Bukidnon as in /liruŋliruŋ/ and /d/ for Talaandig as in /lidənlidən/. These cognates also showed the occurrence of allophonic free variation.

The sixth lexical item is 'dry' which is translated to *'mamara'* /mamara/ in Higaonon, *'mamada'* /mamada/ or *'gangu'* /gaŋu/ in Talaandig, and *'mamara'* /mamara/ in Bukidnon. While Higaonon and Bukidnon share the same translation for the word *'dry'* which is *'mamara'* /mamara/, Talaandig differs since it makes use of *'mamada'* /mamada/ or *'gangu'* /gaŋu/. Talaandig in this case still prefers the phoneme /d/ while Higaonon and Bukidnon prefer the phoneme /r/. This is another proof that allophonic free variation occurred in these varieties.

The eight lexical item is 'name' which is equivalent to *'ngaran'* /ŋaran/ in Higaonon, *'ngaran'* /ŋaran/ or *'ngadan'* /ŋadan/ in Talaandig, and *'ngaran'* /ŋaran/ in Bukidnon. Notice that all three Binukid varieties adopt the term *'ngaran'* /ŋaran/ but Talaandig has another alternative word for it which is *'ngadan'* /ŋadan/. All phonemes are the same in the three cognates except that Talaandig used the phoneme /d/ in its alternative word *'ngadan'* /ŋadan/ which also reveal the allophoic free variation phenomenon.

The ninth lexical item is 'dog' which is translated in Higaonon as *'asu'* /asu/, in Talaandig as *'aso'* /asɔ/, and in Bukidnon as *'asu'* /asu/. Meanwhile, *'tiyalus'* /tiyalus/ is another word used by Higaonon to refer to 'dog'. It can be observed that Talaandig prefers to use the phoneme /ɔ/ which differs from and Higaonon's and Bukidnon's /u/. Still phonological correspondences occur in these cognates except that Talaandig used the phoneme /ɔ/ as in *'aso'* /asɔ/. This shows that allophonic free variation is also evident in these cognates.

In the lexical item 'louse' which is the tenth lexical item on the table, only Bukidnon differs in terms of the phoneme /i/ in the word *'lisa'* /lisaʔ/ while Higaonon and Talaandig adopt /u/ as in *'lusa'* /lusaʔ/. All phonemes in the three cognates are the same except that Bukidnon preferred to use the phoneme /i/ as in *'lisa'* /lisaʔ/ while Higaonon and Talaandig preferred to use /u/ as in *'lusa'* /lusaʔ/. These cognates still present the occurrence of allophonic free variation.

The eleventh lexical item is 'root'. Its equivalent in Higaonon is *'gamut'* /gamut/, in Talaandig is *'dalid'* /dalid/, and in Bukidnon as *'gamut'* /gamut/. In this case, both Higaonon and Bukidnon share the same terminology while Talaandig preferred a different one. Higaonon and Bukidnon share the same phonetic features while Talaandig adopt different phonemes.

The twelfth lexical item is 'sun' which is translated in Higaonon as *'anlaw'* /anlaʊ/, in Talaandig as *'anlaw'* /anlaʊ/, and in Bukidnon as *'aldaw'* /aldaʊ/. It must be noticed that in this case, only Bukidnon differs among the three varieties. All phonemes of the three cognates are the same except that Bukidnon used the phoneme /d/ instead of /n/. This is another case of allophonic free variation.

The thirteenth lexical item is 'rain' which is *'uran'* /uran/ in Higaonon, *'udan'* /udan/ in Talaandig, and *'uran'* /uran/ in Bukidnon. Both Higaonon and Bukidnon used the word *'uran'* /uran/ while Talaandig preferred the term *'udan'* /udan/. Like in the previous lexica items, all phonemes of the three cognates are the same, except that Talaandig preferred the phoneme /d/ as in *'udan'* /udan/ while Higaonon and Bukidnon preferred the phoneme /r/ as in *'uran'* /uran/. Like in the previous lexical items, these cognates show allophonic free variation.

The word 'earth' which is the fourteenth lexical item on the table is translated in Higaonon as *'kalibutan'* /kalibutan/, in Talaandig as *'kalibutan'* /kalibutan/, and in Bukidnon as *'bugta'* /bugtaʔ/. In this case, only Bukdnon used the term *'bugta'* /bugtaʔ/ while Higaonon and Talaandig preferred the term *'kalibutan'* /kalibutan/. In this case, Higaonon and Talaandig cognates share exactly the same phonemes while Bukdnon cognate used different phonetic features.

The next word is 'cloud' which is the fifteenth lexical item on the table. This term is translated in Higaonon as *'gabunan'* /gabunan/, in Talaandig as *'gabun'* /gabun/, and in Bukidnon as *'gabun'* /gabun/. Notice that only Higaonon used the term *'gabunan'* /gabunan/ while both Talaandig and Bukidnon used the term *'gabun'* /gabun/. It must be noted here that all three cognates share the same phonemes except that Higaonon added a morpheme '-an' for the lexeme *'gabun'* /gabun/ making it *'gabunan'* /gabunan/.

The sixteenth lexical item is 'smoke' which is translated in Higaonon as *'ubel'* /ubəl/ in Higaonon, *'ubul'* /ubul/ in both Talaandig and Bukidnon. What makes the Higaonon cognate different from its equivalent words in Talaandig and Bukidnon is the 'pepet' sound /ə/ in the second syllable of the word *'ubel'* /ubəl/. In this particular phenomenon, Higaonon preferred the use of /ə/ than /u/. Although, all the other phonemes except the /ə/ and /u/ are the same. Allophonic free variation is still evident in these cognates.

The English gloss 'ash' which is the seventeenth lexical item can be translated in Higaonon as *'anuk'* /anuk/ or *'abu'* /abu/, in Talaandig as *'anek'*

/anək/, and in Bukidnon as '*abu*' /abu/. As observed, both Higaonon and Bukidnon used the term '*abu*' /abu/ although Higaonon also used '*anuk*' /anuk/ as an alternative while Talaandig preferred the term '*anek*' /anək/. In this case, phonetic variation occurred for the lexemes '*abu*' /abu/ of Higaonon and Buidnon and the alternative Higaonon lexeme '*anuk*' /anuk/ in terms of /b/ and /n/. Meanwhile, Talaandig preferred to use the phoneme /ə/ as in '*anek*' /anək/ instead of the phoneme /u/ of Higaonon. These cognates still show the occurrence of allophoic free variation.

The next lexical item which is the eighteenth lexical item on the table is 'ear' translated in Higaonon as '*talinga*' /taliŋa/, in Talaandig as '*talinga*' /taliŋa/ or '*tangila*' /taŋila/, and in Bukidnon as '*talinga*' /taliŋa/. In this case, only Talaandig claimed to be using '*tangila*' /taŋila/ as an alternate lexeme for '*talinga*' /taliŋa/. Anyhow, all three cognates share the same phonemes. However, phonetic reversal happened in the cognates '*talinga*' /taliŋa/ and '*tangila*' /taŋila/.

The nineteenth lexical item on the table is 'nose' which is translated in Higaonon as '*irung*' /iruŋ/, in Talaandig as '*ideng*' /idəŋ/, and in Bukidnon as '*idung*' /iduŋ/. It must be noticed however that Higaonon used the phoneme /r/ as in '*irung*' /iruŋ/ instead of /d/ as in '*idung*' /iduŋ/ which is used by Bukidnon. Meanwhile, like Bukidnon, Talaandig preferred /d/ as in '*ideng*' /idəŋ/ but adopts the /ə/ and not the /u/ phoneme. In this case, Talaandig differs in two phonemes while both Higaonon and Bukidnon differs in only one phoneme. Still, allophonic free variation is evident in these cogantes.

The twentieth lexical item is 'tooth' which is equivalent to '*ngipun*' /ŋipun/ in Higaonon, '*ngipen*' /ŋipən/ in Talaandig, and '*ngipun*' /ŋipun/ in Bukidnon. In this lexeme, only Talaandig differs as it adopts the pepet vowel /ə/ as in '*ngipen*' /ŋipən/ while the other varieties do not. Like in the previous lexical items, allophonic free variation is evidet in these cogantes.

The next lexical item which is the twenty second is 'belly' translated in Higaonon as '*getek*' /gətək/, in Talaandig as '*getuk*' /gətuk/, and in Bukidnon as '*getuk*' /gətuk/. In this case, only Higaonon differs in terms of the use of two pepet phonemes /ə/ as in '*getek*' /gətək/ while both Talaandig and Bukidnon shared the exactly the same phonemes. Still, allphoic free variation is shown in these cognateas.

The twenty third lexical item is 'drink' translated in Higaonon as '*inum*' /inum/, in Talaandig as '*inem*' /inəm/, and in Bukidnon as '*inum*' /inum/. It must be noted that both Higaonon and Bukidnon share exactly the same phonemes while Talaandig differs in the use of pepet vowel /ə/ as in /inəm/. This is another incidence of allophoic free variation.

The twenty fourth lexical item is 'sleep' which can be translated as '*tiruga*' /tiruga/ in Higaonon, '*tiduga*' /tiduga/ in Talaandig, and '*tiruga*' /tiruga/ in Bukidnon. Similar with many cases, only Talaandig differs in this case since it adopts the phoneme /d/ in '*tiduga*' /tiduga/ and not the phoneme /r/ which is preferred to be used by both Higaonon and Bukidnon. All the rest of the phonemes are similar. Allophonic free variation is still evident in these cognates.

The twenty fifth lexical item on the table is 'say' translated as '*kagi*' /kagi/ or '*ikagi*' /ikagi/ in Higaonon, '*ikagi*' /ikagi/ or '*ikagihi*' /ikagihi/ in Talaandig, and '*ikagi*' /ikagi/ in Bukidnon. All three varieties used '*ikagi*' /ikagi/ but some alternatives include '*kagi*' /kagi/ of Higaonon and '*ikagihi*' /ikagihi/ in Talaandig. Anyhow, all phonemes are similar in all cognates.

The twenty sixth lexical item on the table is 'kill' translated as '*himatayan*' /himatayan/ in Higaonon, '*himatayan*' /himatayan/ or '*himatayi*' /himatayi/ in Talaandig, and '*himatayi*' /himatayi/ in Bukidnon. It must be noted that only Talaandig used both '*himatayan*' /himatayan/ and '*himatayi*' /himatayi/ while Higaonon used '*himatayan*' /himatayan/ only and Bukidnon used '*himatayi*' /himatayi/. Anyhow, all cognates share the same phonemes.

The twenty seventh lexical item is 'come' which is translated in Higaonon as '*dumini*' /dumini/ or '*dali*' /dali/, in Talaandig as '*dini*' /dini/, and in Bukidnon as '*dini*' /dini/. In this particular instance, only Higaonon differs as it adopts '*dumini*' /dumini/ or '*dali*' /dali/, while both Talaandig and Bukidnon used the lexeme '*dini*' /dini/. It must be noted that a morpheme '-um' is added in the Higaonon cognate '*dumini*' /dumini/. Anyhow, all phonemes in the three cognates are the same except the phoneme /u/ and /m/ of the Higaonon cognate.

The twenty eighth lexical item is 'lie' translated in Higaonon as '*biru*' /biru/, in Talaandig as '*bidu*' /bidu/, and in Bukidnon as '*bidu*' /bidu/. In this particular case, only Higaonon differs as it adopts the phoneme /r/ as in '*biru*' /biru/ while both Talaandig and Bukidnon adopt the phoneme /d/. All the rest of the phonemes of the three cognates are exactly the same. This is another evidence o allophoic free variation.

The twenty ninth lexical item is 'sit' translated in Higaonon as '*panu-u*' /panuʔu/, in Talaandig as '*pinu-u*' /pinuʔu/, and in Bukidnon as '*pinu-u*' /pinuʔu/. Here, only Higaonon differs as it adopts the phoneme /a/ as in '*panu-u*' /panuʔu/ while both Talaandig and Bukidnon adopts the phoneme

/i/ as in '*pinu-u*' /pinuʔu/. All phonemes of the three cognates are the same except the /a/ as in '*panu-u*' /panuʔu/ of the Higaonon and /i/ as in '*pinu-u*' /pinuʔu/ in both Talaandig and Bukidnon. Still, allophonic free variation is evident in these cognates.

The thirtieth lexical item is 'give' translated in Higaonon as '*ila*' /ila/, in Talaandig as '*ila*' /ila/ or '*ilahi*' /ilahi/, and in Bukidnon as '*i-ila*' /iʔila/. It must be noted that both Higaonon and Talaandig used the lexeme '*ila*' /ila/. However, Talaandig used '*ilahi*' /ilahi/ as an alternative lexeme for '*ila*' /ila/ while Bukidnon quietly differs as it adopts the lexeme '*i-ila*' /iʔila/. Anyhow, all phonemes used in these cognates are the same.

The thirty first lexical item is 'black' translated as '*maitum*' /maitum/ in Higaonon, '*maitem*' /maitəm/ in Talaandig, and '*maitum*' /maitum/ in Bukidnon. In here, only Talaandig differs as it used the pepet vowel /ə/ as in '*maitem*' /maitəm/ while both Higaonon and Bukidnon used the phoneme /u/ as in '*maitum*' /maitum/. It must be noted that all three cognates share the same phonemes. Like in many other lexical items previously mentioned, allophonic free variation is shown in these cognates.

The last lexical item on the table is 'night' translated as '*daleman*' /daləman/ in both Higaonon and Talaandig and '*daluman*' /daluman/ in Bukidnon. It must be noted that only Bukidnon differs in terms of the phoneme /u/ as in '*daluman*' /daluman/ while both Higaonon and Talaandig adopt the pepet vowel /ə/ as in '*daleman*' /daləman/. Phonetic similarities occur as well for the rest of the phonemes of the three cognates. This is the last evidence that allophonic free variation is evident in these Binukid cognates.

In general, all three Binukid varieties share similar phonetic features. It must be noticed as well that in many lexical items, Talaandig preferred to use the phoneme /d/ than /r/. Apparently, allophonic free variation is present in these Binukid varieties. Further, the use of the pepet vowel /ə/ is used frequently in the Talaandig cognates compared to the other cognates from different Binukid varieties. This makes Talaandig a slightly different Binukid variety compared to the other two Binukid varieties which are the Higaonon and Bukidnon. This initial finding is strengthened with the use of the Automatic Similarity Judgement Program (ASJP) software which is presented in Table 2.2 below.

The examination of genetic relationship among the three Binukid varieties with the use of the Automatic Similarity Judgement Program (ASJP) software is presented in Table 2.2. The table is divided into three columns: the column for the Binukid Varieties, SIM 100 (in percentage), and SIM 40 (in percentage). Under the Binukid Varieties column are the Binukid varieties paired for comparison such as Higaonon–Talaandig Binukid varieties, Higaonon–Bukidnon Binukid varieties, and Talaandig–Bukidnon varieties. Moreover, SIM 100 means 'similarity' of these varieties based on the Swadesh 100 wordlist. While, SIM 40 means 'similarity' of these varieties based on the Swadesh 40 most stable wordlist. It must be noted that these similarities are expressed in percentage.

Table 2.2: *Percentage of Genetic Relationship of the Three Binukid Varieties using ASJP*

Binukid Varieties	SIM 100 (in percentage)	SIM 40 (in percentage)
Higaonon–Talaandig	84.47	89.15
Higaonon–Bukidnon	98.61	97.56
Talaandig–Bukidnon	84.47	89.15

The table further shows that the three Binukid varieties are definitely related genetically. Based on 100 wordlist, Higaonon and Talaandig Binukid varieties are 84.47 percent related. When tested using the 40 most stable wordlist, Higaonon and Talaandig Binukid varieties are 89.15 percent related.

Furthermore, the same percentage is accounted for the Talaandig and Bukidnon Binukid varieties. Based on 100 wordlist, Talaandig and Bukidnon Binukid varieties are 84.47 percent related and 89.15 percent related based on the 40 most stable wordlist of Swadesh.

Finally, when Higaonon and Bukidnon Binukid varieties were compared in their similarities, it revealed that these varieties are 98.61 percent related based on Swadesh 100 wordlist, and 97.56 percent related based on the 40 most stable wordlist by Swadesh. It goes to say that Higaonon and Bukidnon varieties are much related with each other compared to Higaonon–Talaandig and Bukidnon–Talaandig pairs.

The Time-Depth (Year of Divergence) of these Language Varieties

Shown in Table 2.3 is the time depth or year of divergence of the three Binukid varieties. Time depth is often called 'year of divergence'. This refers to the point in time when languages diverged or split from each other.

Table 2.3: *Time Depth (Year of Divergence) of the Three Binukid Varieties*

Binukid Varieties	Time Depth or Language Divergence (in years)
Higaonon–Talaandig	48
Higaonon–Bukidnon	0
Talaandig–Bukidnon	48

Based on the table, Higaonon and Talaandig Binukid varieties the same with Talaandig and Bukidnon varieties gradually split from each other in the past 48 years as of the moment of this writing. Meanwhile, no time depth or language divergence was detected between Higaonon and Bukidnon varieties most likely because of their high degree of relatedness (98.61 percent in SIM 100, 97.56 percent in SIM 40) as shown in Table 2.

The Phylogenetic Classification of these Language Varieties

Phylogenetic classification refers to the classification of languages based on their genetic relationship plotted through an illustration. After a thorough analysis on the genetic relationship of languages, a phylogenetic classification could be formed based on the similarity and time depth of the languages under study.

It is already a fact that Philippine languages including the Binukid language belongs to the following family line: Austronesian, Malayo-Polynesian, Greater Central Philippines, Manobo, North Manobo, and Kinamiguin–Bukidnon. Further, the Binukid language in the Bukidnon province spoken by the Higaonon, Talaandig, and Bukidnon tribes are under the parent language group Kinamiguin–Bukidnon.

The phylogenetic classification by SIL through Ethnologue is more detailed since it shows other language groups that belong to the Austronesian language family. It must be noted however that in Ethnologue only Higaonon and Talaandig Binukid are shown leaving the Bukidnon Binukid variety uncounted. This is the inconsistency that I would want to address through my proposed phylogenetic classification.

Based on the analysis on the genetic relationship among the Higaonon, Talaandig, and Bukidnon Binukid varieties, I am able to come up with a proposed phylogenetic classification of these languages as shown below. The Binukid language varieties under study are enclosed with a circle. This phylogenetic classification was already checked by my data analyst Eric W. Holman.

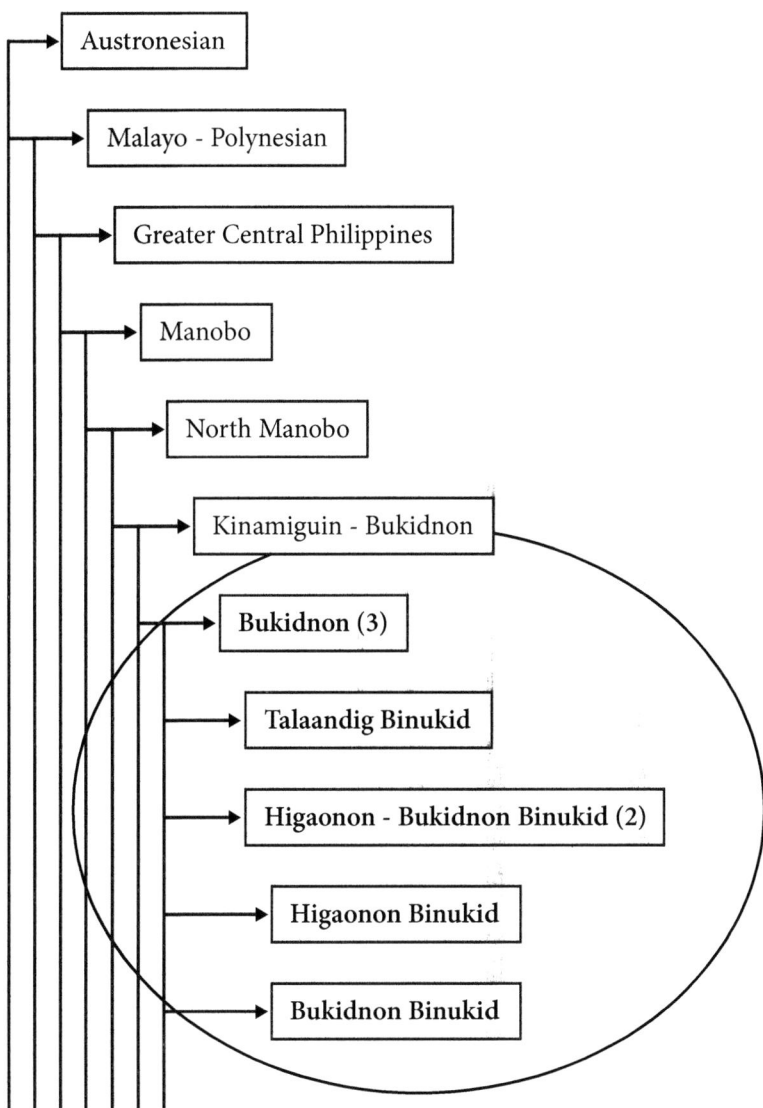

Figure 1. Proposed Correction on the Phylogenetic Classification of the Binukid Language by SIL through Ethnologue

Meanwhile, in my proposed phylogenetic classification, I only included the language groups to which the Binukid language directly descended from (*Austronesian, Malayo-Polynesian, Greater Central Philippines, Manobo, North Manobo, Kinamiguin–Bukidnon, and Bukidnon*).

Focusing on the Binukid language, it must be noted that of the three Binukid varieties under study, Talaandig Binukid variety branched off first from the other two varieties which are the Higaonon and Bukidnon Binukid Varieties. This is implied by the percentage of similarity between Higaonon and Bukidnon Binukid varieties which is 98.61 percent in SIM 100 and 97.56 percent in SIM 40. It must be noted that the Talaandig Binukid variety is only 84.47 percent and 89.15 percent related to Higaonon and Bukidnon Binukid varieties in SIM 100 and SIM 40 respectively. This analysis on the genetic relationship of these Binukid language varieties suggests that Talaandig Binukid variety diverged or split from the Higaonon and Bukidnon Binukid varieties in 48 years as of the moment of this writing.

Furthermore, this phylogenetic classification on Binukid language is an attempt to correct the existing phylogenetic classification by Ethnologue, a project by the Summer Institute of Linguistics (SIL) that presents the classification of the languages in the world including the Binukid language. Below is the present phylogenetic classification of the Binukid language by SIL through Ethnologue which I intend to correct using my proposed phylogenetic classification.

In summary, the socio–demographic profile of the informants revealed that most of them are females that belong to the age bracket 60–65 years old. Six of them are from the Higaonon tribe, six from the Talaandig tribe, and another six from the Bukidon tribe. The other language mostly spoken by the informants is Cebuano aside from the Binukid language. Lastly, most respondents reached elementary level in terms of their highest educational attainment.

The analysis on the genetic relationship of these three Binukid language varieties revealed that Higaonon and Bukidnon Binukid varieties are much related with each other as suggested by the percentage of similarity of 98.61 percent in SIM 100 and 97.56 in SIM 40. Meanwhile, Talaandig and Higaonon and Talaandig and Bukidnon only share 84.47 percent similarity based on SIM 100 and 89.15 percent based on SIM 40. Below is a diagram showing the genetic relationship among the three Binukid language varieties.

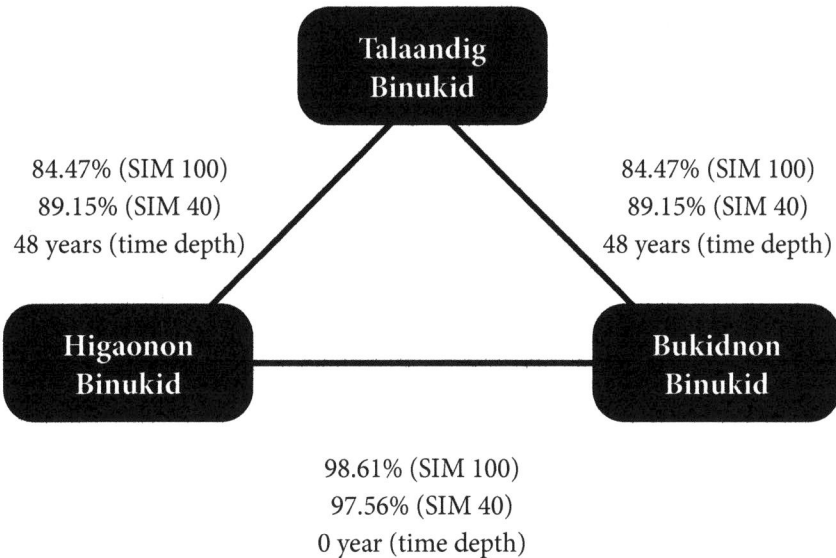

Figure 2. Diagram on the Genetic Relationship among the Binukid language varieties

Furthermore, the analysis on time depth or language divergence revealed that Talaandig Binukid variety branched off first from the Higaonon and Bukidnon Binukid varieties in the past 48 years.

CHAPTER 5
DISCUSSION

Presented in this chapter are the discussions, implications for practice, implications for future research and the concluding remarks.

This study is conducted to address the inconsistencies on the reports of the Binukid language. As mentioned in the chapter 1 and 2, there is an inconsistency on the records of Binukid language. This language is believed to be spoken by the seven tribal groups who first inhabited the province. Three of these seven tribal groups include the Higaonon, Talaandig, and Bukidnon tribes. The inconsistency started when the now–defunct Presidential Assistant for National Minorities (PANAMIN) as reported by Thomas (2000) and Industan (2009), an academician and a native Bukidnon classified the Binukid into three varieties spoken by the Higaonon, Talaandig, and the Bukidnon tribe. These classifications suggest that the other four tribal groups are not Binukid speakers in contrast with the belief of the people in the province.

However, Elkins (1974) in his glottochronological works reported that Binukid is only spoken by the Higaonon and Talaandig tribes which simply imply that Bukidnon tribe is not a Binukid–speaking group as claimed by Thomas (2000) in PANAMIN and Industan (2009). In addition, the Bukidnon provincial government website contributed to the existing inconsistency as it stated that Binukid is the dialect of the Bukidnon tribal group. It never stated that the same Binukid is spoken by the Higaonon and Talaandig tribal groups.

Moreover, the Summer Institute of Linguistics International (SIL International) through its project called Ethnologue, presented that Binukid is a sister language of Higaonon, Kagayanen, and Manobo (Simons & Fennig, 2018). This claim challenges the works of Elkins (1974) who classified that Manobo is the mother language of Binukid, and that Binukid is spoken by the Higaonon people.

Given these inconsistencies, I am motivated to conduct an investigation on the genetic relationship of the Binukid language varieties particularly the Higaonon, Talaandig, and Bukidnon Binukid varieties by examining its phonological variations and similarities with the employment of the

Automated Similarity Judgement Program (ASJP). Moreover, there are no other lexicostatistical studies conducted on these Binukid language varieties. Thus, I am encouraged to pursue this study with the hope that I can address this inconsistency and eventually contribute to the limited body of literature on the relationship of these Binukid language varieties.

The Socio-Demographic Profile of the Informants

The socio-demographic profile is considered to be important in this study. Looking into the background of the informants would give any researcher a glimpse on some factors that could possibly affect the data gathered. In this study, I checked on the following profiles: age, dialect spoken, other languages spoken, and highest educational attainment.

Age is one factor considered in this study since it is believed to have an effect on the responses of the informants. When talking about utterances, the elderly are found to have depth in their reflections compared to the younger ones. The elderly are observed to have a profound knowledge on a lot of issues asked to them (Knauper et al., 2016).

In this study, I personally chose the elderly whose age ranges from 60 years old and above since I believed that they could provide more accurate translations of words, from their native language to another as older adults tend to have larger vocabularies and greater lexical knowledge compared to younger adults (Alwin & McCammon, 2001; Verhaeghen, 2003; Juncos-Rabadan et al., 2005; Rossi & Diaz, 2016). Most likely, the elderly use their native tongue often during communicative activities like speaking and writing compared to their young counterparts. They usually use their native language especially when talking to their children, grandchildren, and their peers. Based on this premise, I would say that they are more knowledgeable in terms of translation from their native tongue to the target language and thus, making them best fit in this study.

There were eighteen informants who answered the instrument of this study. Six informants were from the Higaonon tribe, six from the Talaandig tribe, and another six from the Bukidnon tribe who translated the Swadesh wordlist into their native language which is Binukid. Of the six, three translated the wordlist. These three were also asked to read the wordlist as I recorded it for me to know the phonetic features of the words. Meanwhile, the other three were tasked to participate during the focus group discussion. The purpose of the focus group discussion is to verify and triangulate the responses of the first three who translated the wordlist through writing. These three also verified whether the wordlist are correctly pronounced by the first three informants. It is very important for me to get the correct pronunciation of the wordlist so I could transcribe it into sound symbols using the International Phonetic Alphabet (IPA) and eventually using the ASJP codes. These codes are important since these will be fed to the ASJP software for the analysis of the genetic relationship of the three Binukid language varieties. It must also be noted that I intended to come up with an equal number of informants from each tribe. Six informants were invited to participate in the study from each tribal group. This is to assure that the three tribal groups are equally represented to prevent possible issues of bias in terms of informants' representation.

Moreover, Cebuano is revealed as the other major language mostly spoken by the informants. In other words, Cebuano is the lingua franca used particularly in the communities where the Higaonon, Talaandig, and Bukidnon people settled. It must be noted that the Higaonon people in this study came from Sumilao, Bukidnon while the Talaandig in this study came from Kibangay, Lantapan, Bukidnon. On the other hand, the Bukidnon people who participated in this study came from Casisang, Malaybalay City. Other languages spoken by the informants were English and Filipino.

I intended to include the other languages spoken by the informants since I consider these as relevant in my study. The linguistic competence of informants in other languages may affect their knowledge on their native tongue. In this case, informants may find it challenging when asked to translate vocabularies from Cebuano for example, to their native tongue which is Binukid. This phenomenon is called crosslinguistic influence, when the second language interferes or somehow affects the first language or vice versa (Weinrich, 1953; Lado, 1968; Ilomaki, 2005; Magno, 2017).

Moreover, the study of Kaushanskaya et al. (2011) suggests that our native language competency can be affected by our second language competency which can either facilitate or reduce our performance in the native language. Marian and Spivey (2003) substantiated this finding as they claimed in their study that our knowledge on the second language influences our ability to manage information in our native tongue.

The last indicator under the socio-demographic profile in this study is the highest educational attainment. Educational attainment of the informants may affect as well to the accuracy of translations of the wordlist. It is believed that the more educated the informants are, the more they are contaminated already with the second language they learned. Meaning, there would be a tendency that the informants will no longer remember the exact translations of words since they are already accustomed to using their second language. In reverse, it is assumed that the less educated the person is, the lesser the tendency that he becomes contaminated with the second language.

This is best explained using the lens of the first–language attrition phenomenon when at some point a second language learner undergoes a process of language loss, forgetting, and deterioration in his first language as he learned a second language (Schmid, 2008). Overseas Filipino Workers (OFWs) for example would find it difficult to return speaking their mother tongue as they learned a second language in a foreign country.

However, Levy et al. (2007), preferred to use the word 'inhibition' than 'forgetfulness'. They claimed that we tend to actively inhibit words in our native language as these distract us as we speak our second language. In other words, it is not because we use less our native tongue that we forget it. The state of forgetfulness may actually be a helpful technique for people to learn a second language better. In whatever way we define language attrition, still educational attainment of informants plays a crucial part in this study as it potentially affects the stock of vocabularies of the informants.

The present study revealed that the most informants reached elementary level followed by elementary graduates and high school graduates. These are followed by college level and college graduates and then high school level. Since most of the informants only reached elementary level, I think it is safe to conclude that they are less contaminated with other languages spoken around. This makes them fit to become informants of the study.

Genetic Relationship of the Higaonon, Talaandig, and Bukidnon Binukid Varieties

Genetic relationship or genealogical relationship of languages are usually examined by historical linguists to prove the relatedness of languages that are believed to be (or the otherwise) descendants of the same language family. Genetic relationship between and among languages are conventionally examined using lexicostatistics and glottochronology.

Lexicostatistics was formulated by Morris Swadesh as a methodology in studying vocabulary statistically to determine degrees of genetic relationship between and among languages based on the number of cognates present the languages under study (Hymes, 1960). On the other hand, glottochronology has always been associated with lexicostatistics since it deals in particular with phylogenetic relationship among languages (Campbell, 2013). Glottochronology utilizes the frequency of the cognancy found using lexicostatistics to determine language depth (or language divergence). Using glottochronology, one could determine language depth and eventually subgrouping of previously not known to be related languages. Thus, glottochronology is always considered as an extension of lexicostatistics.

The emergence of lexicostatistics and glottochronology has ignited doubts and questions on the validity of these linguistic methodologies. And so, contemporary historical linguists came up with a modern technique to determine language relationships and trace back time depth or language divergence. One modern method is through the use of the ASJP software created by a group of linguists, anthropologists, and psychologists. ASJP means Automated Similarity Judgement Program designed to examine genealogical relationship, time depth, and subgrouping of languages through algorithm and complex computer programing. Since it is automated, it is more objective compared to the conventional lexicostatistics and glottochronology.

In this study, I investigated on the genetic relationship of the three Binukid language varieties such as Higaonon, Talaandig, and Binukid language varieties. By examining the phonological variations and correspondences of the three Binukid varieties, it revealed that Talaandig slightly differed from the other two Binukid varieties. Two evidences can prove this: first, in most lexemes, Talaandig preferred the phoneme /d/ than /r/ which is preferred instead by both Higaonon and Bukidnon varieties; second, it is observed in many instances that Taalaandig preferred the pepet vowel /ə/ than /u/ which is preferred rather by the Higaonon and Bukidnon varieties.

With the use of ASJP, the study revealed that all these three Binukid language varieties are definitely related genetically. Specifically, Higaonon and Bukidnon Binukid varieties are much related with each other compared to the pairs Talaandig–Higaonon and Talaandig–Bukidnon Binukid language varieties. This finding implies that these three Binukid varieties are descendants of the same language family. They are sister languages as suggested by the high percentage of similarities found after these Binukid varieties are examined in their genealogical relationship.

Moreover, this finding is imperative since it confirms the claims of Thomas (2000) in PANAMIN and Industan (2009) that the Binukid language is commonly spoken by the Higaonon, Talaandig, and Bukidnon tribal groups. In addition, it validates the belief of the people of Bukidnon that these three tribal groups share the same mother tongue.

One significant implication of the findings is that it rejects the claims of Elkins (1974) in his glottochronological works that Binukid is only spoken by the Higaonon and Talaandig tribes which simply implies that Bukidnon tribe is not a Binukid-speaking group. Furthermore, the finding also elucidates the existing inconsistency in the Bukidnon provincial government website that only declared Binukid as the dialect of the Bukidnon tribal group leaving the Higaonon and Talaandig uncounted.

Likewise, this finding rejects the claims of Summer Institute of Linguistics International (SIL International) through its project called Ethnologue, that Binukid is a sister language of Higaonon, together with Kagayanen, and Manobo (Simons & Fennig, 2018). The reality is, Binukid is a language spoken by the Higaonon people. Finally, it is with much hope that this proof of genetic relatedness of the Higaonon, Talaandig, and Bukidnon Binukid varieties will become a solid basis to correct these existing errors and inconsistencies on the record and reports about the Binukid language in textbooks, research articles, blogs, and websites. May this finding be used to enrich the teaching and strengthen the literature on the language ancestry of Binukid.

Time-Depth or Language Divergence of the Higaonon, Talaandig, and Bukidnon Binukid Varieties

Time depth or language divergence refers to the point in time when languages split or separated from each other or from their parent language. It is believed that when languages separate from their parent language, new words arise while others are replaced, meanings evolve, grammar morphs, sounds change, and speech communities diverged into dialects and then become distinct languages (Gray et al., 2011).

Time depth or language divergence can be determined based on the degree of relatedness of the languages under study. In the present study, the estimated time depths for the Higaonon, Talaandig, and Bukidnon Binukid varieties are low given their high percentage of similarities or relatedness.

Since Higaonon and Bukidnon Binukid varieties are much similar, no time depth or language divergence is found. Meaning, these two Binukid varieties have not diverged from each other as of yet. In other words, the Binukid variety spoken by the Higaonon people in Sumilao, Bukidon are almost exactly the same with the Binukid variety spoken by the Bukidnon people in Casisang, Malaybalay City. Though geographically distant from each other, the Binukid varieties they speak are still intact as one Binukid dialect.

However, given its lower percentage of similarity with the other two Binukid varieties, Talaandig was found to have branched off first from the other two Binukid varieties in 48 years. This divergence is most likely attributed to a lot of factors including the split of Binukid–speaking communities from time immemorial. This split is evident at present since Talaandig tribal group settled themselves away from Malaybalay area where Bukidnon tribal group are mostly found. They settled in the Municipalities of Kibangay and Lantapan. On the other hand, Higaonon people are located in Sumilao and in some areas in North Bukidnon.

So when a language split into dialects new words arise while others are replaced, meanings evolve, sounds change, and grammar morphs making these languages distinct dialects from a common origin (Gray et al., 2011). Over a long period of time, sound changes happened in the Binukid language as its speakers dispersed in different places in the province. For example, Talaandig Binukid speakers preferred the word '*daduwa*' while Higaonon and Bukidnon Binukid speakers preferred the word '*daruwa*' which means 'two'. The same phenomenon in the case of '*adagi*' (big) for Talaandig Binukid speakers and '*aragi*' (big) for both the Higaonon and Bukidnon Binukid speakers.

This finding implies that the Binukid language just like any other language is affected by external factors causing the divergence of the Talaandig Binukid variety. It is on this premise that I could infer that the Talaandig Binukid variety will become a very distinct variety of Binukid in the years to come given that it constantly diverges from the other two Binukid varieties as years pass by. Follow up longitudinal studies might also be conducted every ten years from now on to assess whether the rate of the language divergence of the Talaandig Binukid variety is constant. These studies may also evaluate whether the other Binukid varieties have started splitting from each other.

Conducting researches on genetic relationship and language divergence today would definitely help linguists of the far future generations to come up with accurate phylogenetic classifications of languages. With these types of studies, linguists would be able to reconstruct language classifications even among those languages that are dying and those that are newly born.

The Phylogenetic Classification of the Higaonon, Talaandig, and Bukidnon Binukid Varieties

Phylogenetic classification refers to the sorting of languages based on their genetic relationship with each other and time depth plotted on a diagram. Basically, a phylogenetic classification is a language tree that shows the phylogeny of a language from the parent language(s) it descended from and to its daughter language or group of languages.

Based on the analysis of the genetic relationship among the Higaonon, Talaandig, and Bukidnon Binukid varieties, Talaandig variety branched off first from the other two varieties in 48 years as of the moment of this writing. This finding is based on the percentage of similarities and relatedness of the three Binukid varieties.

Since Higaonon and Bukidnon Binukid varieties are almost exactly the same given their high percentage of similarity in SIM 100 and in SIM 40, these varieties are considered to be an intact one Binukid dialect though spoken by two geographically distant tribal groups. One is from Sumilao, Bukidnon and the other is from Casisang, Malaybalay City.

However, since Talaandig Binukid is found to have a lower similarity percentage when paired with Higaonon Binukid and Bukidnon Binukid, it is found to have diverged from the other two varieties in the recent 48 years. This finding implies a different phylogeny for the Talaandig Binukid variety. In simpler words, another phylogenetic branch will be assigned to Talaandig Binukid variety leaving the Higaonon and Bukidnon Binukid varieties in the same branch.

The phylogenetic classifications of these languages in descending order will now appear as follows: Austronesian, Malayo-Polynesian, Greater Central Philippines, Manobo, North Manobo, Kinamiguin-Bukidnon, and then Bukidnon which composed the Talaandig Binukid and Higaonon-Bukidnon Binukid. Lastly, the Higaonon-Bukidnon Binukid is further composed of the Higaonon Binukid and the Bukidnon Binukid.

Finally, this phylogenetic classification is a new contribution to the existing phylogenetic classifications done by SIL International through its Ethnologue. It must be noted that in the present classification of the Binukid language, Higaonon was assigned a different ISO code (mba) while Talaandig is considered as a dialect of Binukid (bkd). Ethnologue failed to present evidence for this classification considering that not much is known about these based on their descriptions. Glottology does not even mention Bukidnon as one Binukid variety.

With this finding, I hope that I would be able to clarify inconsistencies and correct errors on the records and reports about the Binukid language, its varieties, and phylogeny. As a practicing linguist and a citizen of the Bukidnon province, I feel the duty to know more about this language so I would be able to educate the young Bukidnons on the beauty and grandeur of this ethnic language. In this simple way, I would be able to inculcate rekindle appreciation and cultivate pride in their hearts on their cultural and linguistic heritage. This might help preserve the Binukid language for a lifetime.

Implications for Practice

The main objective of this study is to confirm whether the Higaonon Binukid, Talaandig Binukid, and Bukidnon Binukid varieties are genetically related languages. In this way, I would be able to validate existing beliefs about the language and somehow correct inconsistencies on the records and reports of this language.

To help me achieve this objective, I sought help from Eric W. Holman, a Professor Emeritus from the University of California, Los Angeles, and a member of a group of psychologists, linguists, anthropologists, and computer scientists who created the Automated Similarity Judgement Program (ASJP). This program was especially designed through a rigid algorithm and computer programming to examine genetic relationship and time depth or language divergence which become the bases to construct or reconstruct the phylogenetic classifications of languages.

The findings in this study revealed that the Binukid varieties such as the Higaonon Binukid, Talaandig Binukid, and Bukidnon Binukid are definitely related genetically. It was found that Higaonon and Bukidnon Binukid varieties are more related compared to the Higaonon-Talaandig pair and Talaandig–Bukidnon pair. Further, the data analysis revealed that Talaandig branched off first in the recent 48 years from the Higaonon and Bukidnon Binukid varieties given its low similarity percentage with the other two Binukid varieties.

These findings posit several implications. First, it is proven in this study that these Binukid varieties are descendants of the same language family. With this, it validates the common belief of people in Bukidnon that these Binukid varieties share a common mother tongue. Moreover, it confirms the claims of Thomas (2000) in PANAMIN and Industan (2009) that the Binukid language is commonly spoken by the Higaonon, Talaandig, and Bukidnon tribal groups.

Likewise, it elucidates existing inconsistencies about this language as reported by Elkins (1974), the statements in the Bukidnon provincial government website, and the claims of Summer Institute of Linguistics International (SIL International). After knowing the genetic relatedness of these Binukid varieties, after correcting all the inconsistencies on the reports of this language, the common question then will be 'so what?'.

At the academic level, the findings would somehow educate the academic community especially in the province of Bukidnon on the real identity of the Binukid language. The inconsistencies on the report of this language on textbooks, research articles, blogs, websites, and other platforms would be elucidated and corrected. With this, teachers, students, and all the members in the academic community will have a common understanding about the Binukid language, its varieties, and its phylogeny.

In addition, the proof of genetic relatedness of these three Binukid varieties will strengthen the cultural and linguistic identity of the Higaonon, Talaandig, and Bukidnon people. Eventually, it is possible to cultivate a sense of pride in the hearts of the Binukid speakers on their cultural and linguistic heritage. Thus, they would continue speaking Binukid with pride and subsequently preserve the language for a lifetime. At the political level, upon knowing the proof of genetic relatedness of these Binukid varieties, provincial officials in the province of Bukidnon may initiate programs and ordinances that may underscore the use and preservation of the Binukid language.

To sum it up, may these findings be used to strengthen the identity of the Binukid language, foster appreciation and cultivate a sense of pride in the hearts of the Binukid speakers towards its lifetime preservation. It is with fervent hope that the finding of this research endeavor would enrich the teaching of Binukid language and its ancestry.

Thus, I as the researcher, intends to present the result of this study to the academic community and the officials of the provincial government in Bukdnon to validate to them that these three Binukid language varieties are truly related genetically. And, that Talaandig Binukid variety is gradually branching off from the other two varieties. This will inform the officials of the province of Bukidnon and elucidate inconsistencies and errors on the report of the Binukid language circulating in the academic community of the province.

Implications for Future Research

This research endeavor has paved a way for the conduct of more linguistic investigations focusing on genetic relationship, time depth or language divergence, and the subgrouping of languages or phylogenetic classifications.

Personally, after completing this research study, I extend this linguistic inquiry on the remaining four tribal groups in Bukidnon who also claimed to be Binukid speakers. These remaining four tribal groups include: Manobo, Matigsalug, Umayamnon, and Tigwahanon.

Bukidnon takes pride as the home of the seven ethnic groups who originally inhabited the province from the time unknown. And so, if I could study the genetic relationship and time depth or language divergence of these seven Binukid varieties, I intend to construct a phylogenetic classification of these Binukid varieties. In this way, I may unveil the linguistic identities of these seven tribes thus enriching the cultural and linguistic heritage of the province.

A follow up study may also be conducted on the genetic relationship of Tagalog, Bikolano, and Ilokano to validate the findings of Nelson in 2001. It must be noted that Nelson (2001) examined the genetic relationship of these languages in Northern, Central, and Southern Luzon using the conventional methods of lexicostatistics and glottochronology. Results showed that these languages descended from a common language family. Meanwhile, Ilokano and Bikolano split from Tagalog at an equal rate. Individually, Ilokano and Bikolano are equally more related to Tagalog than to each other.

A similar study may also be conducted among the Manobo group of languages. This research endeavor will definitely require a wider coverage considering the dispersion of all Manobo tribal groups in different locations. However, when this is pursued, this validates or invalidates the Proto–Manobo Theory of Elkins (1974). A study may also be conducted among the Cebuano, Hiligaynon, and Karay-a languages. This is to confirm the common belief that these three languages are genetically related under the Visayan (alternate spelling: Bisayan) Group of languages (Simons & Fennig, 2018).

Another may also be conducted on the genetic relationship among Cebuano, Hiligaynon, and Tagalog languages to validate the claims of Wolfenden (1972) that these three languages are closely related. Lastly, similar studies may also be conducted using other contemporary methodologies aside from the Automated Similarity Judgement Program (ASJP) for comparison of results.

Concluding Remarks

As I finished the conduct of this study, I realized some vital points that widened my horizon as a neophyte in linguistic inquiries.

First, correcting inconsistencies in the reports of the Binukid language is a big deal. At the personal level, it gives me a morale boost as a neophyte in linguistic researches. It gives me enthusiasm to research more on this language so I could contribute for a better understanding of this language.

Second, investigations on genetic relationship of languages need a keen listening skill especially on the phonetic makeup of the wordlist. It needs a careful attention on sound transcription and ASJP coding since these are the data needed for the analysis of the languages under study.

Third, the genetic relatedness of Higaonon, Talaandig, and Bukidnon Binukid varieties can potentially correct present inconsistencies about this language. With this, I hope that the findings of this study will cascade throughout different print platforms like textbooks, research articles, blogs, and websites so more people will be informed.

Fourth, I am amazed knowing the fact that at present, it is already possible to examine genetic relationship of languages with the use of a more objective contemporary methods like the employment of Automated Similarity Judgement Program (ASJP). This innovation could open doors to more linguistic studies on genetic relationship of languages.

Finally, I would not have been able to complete this study alone. Thus, I am forever grateful to Eric W. Holman and his team for his untiring effort for the analysis of my data. Holman has always been willing to answer my queries though he does not know me personally. I am forever grateful as well to my adviser in the University of Mindanao, my informants, gatekeepers of the three tribal groups, and the barangay officials who helped me conduct this study. This research endeavor has become fulfilling and exciting with the help of these wonderful people.

REFERENCES

Alwin, D. F., & McCammon, R. J. (2001). Aging, cohorts, and verbal ability. *The Journals of Gerontology Series B: Psychological Sciences and Social Sciences, 56*(3), 151-161.

Anney, V. N. (2014). Ensuring the quality of the findings of qualitative research: Looking at trustworthiness criteria. *Journal of Emerging Trends in Educational Research and Policy Studies (JETERAPS), 5*(2), 272-281.

Baxter, W. H., & Ramer, A. M. (2000). Beyond lumping and splitting: Probabilistic issues in historical linguistics. *Time depth in historical linguistics, 1*, 167-188.

Bell, E., & Bryman, A. (2007). The ethics of management research: An exploratory content analysis. *British Journal of Management, 18*(1), 63-77.

Bergsland, K., & Vogt, H. (1962). On the validity of glottochronology. *Current Anthropology, 3*(2), 115-153.

Bitsch, V. (2005). Qualitative research: A grounded theory example and evaluation criteria. *Journal of Agribusiness, 23*(345-2016-15096), 75-91.

Bowern, C. (2015). *Linguistic fieldwork: A practical guide.* Switzerland. Springer.

Braff, J. (2010). Conflicts of interest in research — Towards a greater Transparency. *The Permanente Journal, 14*(2). https://doi.org/10.7812/TPP/10-057

Campbell, L. (2013). *Historical linguistics.* Edinburgh: Edinburgh University Press.

Comrie, B. (2005). *The world atlas of language structures.* England: Oxford University Press.

Creswell, J. W., & Creswell, J. D. (2017). *Research design: Qualitative, quantitative, and mixed methods approaches.* Newbury Park, California: Sage Publications.

Cruttenden, A. (2014). *Gimson's pronunciation of English.* Oxfordshire: Routledge.

Dolgopolsky, A. B. (1986). A probabilistic hypothesis concerning the oldest relationships among the language families of northern Eurasia. *Typology, Relationship and Time: A collection of papers on language change and relationship by Soviet linguists*, 27-50.

Dyen, I. (1962). The lexicostatistical classification of the Malayopolynesian languages. *Language, 38*(1), 38. https://doi.org/10.2307/411187

Elkins, R. E. (1974). A Proto-Manobo word list. *Oceanic linguistics, 13*(1/2), 601-641.

Geisler, H., & List, J. M. (2009). Beautiful trees on unstable ground. *Notes on the data problem in lexicostatistics. Presentation held at the Arbeitstagung der Indogermanischen Gesellschaft.*

Gray, R. D., Atkinson, Q. D., & Greenhill, S. J. (2011). Language evolution and human history: What a difference a date makes. *Philosophical Transactions of the Royal Society of London B: Biological Sciences, 366*(1567), 1090–1100. https://doi.org/10.1098/RSTB.2010.0378

Greenberg, J. H. (1993). Observations concerning Ringe's" Calculating the Factor of Chance in Language Comparison". *Proceedings of the American Philosophical Society, 137*(1), 79-90.

Guba, E. G. (1981). Criteria for assessing the trustworthiness of naturalistic inquiries. *Ectj, 29*(2), 75.

Gudschinsky, S. C. (1955). Lexico-statistical skewing from dialect borrowing. *International Journal of American Linguistics, 21*(2), 138-149.

Gudschinsky, S. C. (1956). The ABC's of lexicostatistics (glottochronology). *Word, 12*(2), 175-210. https://doi.org/10.1080/00437956.1956.11659599

Harmon, C. J. W. (2007). *Kagayanen and the Manobo subgroup of Philippine languages* (Doctoral dissertation, UMI Ann Arbor). Retrieved from http://hdl.handle.net/11858/00-001M-0000-0012-870B-C

Heggarty, P. (2010). Beyond lexicostatistics: how to get more out of 'word list'comparisons. *Diachronica, 27*(2), 301-324.

Hoijer, H. (1956). Lexicostatistics: A critique. *Language, 32*(1), 49-60.

Holman, E. W., Wichmann, S., Brown, C. H., Velupillai, V., Müller, A., & Bakker, D. (2008). Explorations in automated language classification. *Folia Linguistica, 42*(3-4), 331-354.

Huang, B. F. (1997). Range and standard for defining comparative cognate lists: An example for Sino-Tibetan languages. *Min. Lang. China 4*, 10–16.

Hymes, D. (1970). Morris Swadesh. https://doi.org/10.1080/00437956.1970.11435588

Hymes, D. H. (1960). Lexicostatistics so far. *Current Anthropology, 1*(1), 3-44. Retrieved from https://www.jstor.org/stable/2739673?seq=2#metadata_info_tab_contents

Ilomaki, A. (2005). Cross-linguistic influence–A cross-sectional study with particular reference to Finnish-speaking and English-speaking learners of German. *UnpublishedB. A thesis). Trinity College, Dublin.*

Industan, E. M. (2009). *Tribes, languages, and dialects: The Bukidnon case.* [Blog post]. Retrieved from http://edmund-industan.blogspot.com/2009/06/tribes-languages-dialects-bukidnon-case.html

International Committee of Medical Journal Editors. (2017). Defining the role of authors and contributors. ICMJE website.

Jäger, G., & Wichmann, S. (2016). Inferring the world tree of languages from word lists. In *The Evolution of Language: Proceedings of the 11th International Conference (EVOLANGX11)*, Online at http://evolang.org/neworleans/papers/147.html.

Jassem, Z. A. & Campbell. (2013). *Historical linguistics: A critical review.* Retrieved from https://www.academia.edu

Jiang, D. (2007). *On evolutionary models of sound changes for Sino-Tibetan languages: Theores and methods of historical linguistics.* Beijing: Social Science Academy Press.

Juncos-Rabadán, O., Pereiro, A. X., & Rodríguez, M. S. (2005). Narrative speech in aging: Quantity, information content, and cohesion. *Brain and Language, 95*(3), 423-434.

Kaushanskaya, M., Yoo, J., & Marian, V. (2011). The effect of second-language experience on native-language processing. *Vigo International Journal of Applied Linguistics*, 8, 54.

Kessler, B. (2001). *The significance of word lists: Statistical tests for investigating historical connections between languages.* Stanford, CA: CSLI Publications.

Knäuper, B., Carrière, K., Chamandy, M., Xu, Z., Schwarz, N., & Rosen, N. O. (2016). How aging affects self-reports. *European Journal of Ageing, 13*(2), 185–193. doi:10.1007/s10433-016-0369-0

Koehn, P., & Knight, K. (2001). Knowledge sources for word-level translation models. In *Proceedings of the 2001 Conference on Empirical Methods in Natural Language Processing.*

Lado, R. (1968). *Linguistics across cultures: Applied linguistics for language teachers. With a Foreword by Charles C. Fries.* Michigan, USA: University of Michigan Press.

Lees, R. B. (1953). The basis of glottochronology. *Language,* 113-127.

Li, P. J. K. (1995). "Is Chinese genetically related to Austronesian?" in *The Ancestry of the Chinese Language,* ed W. S-Y. Wang (Berkeley, CA: Project on Linguistics Analysis), 93–112.

Lincoln, Y. S., & Guba, E. G. (1986). But is it rigorous? Trustworthiness and authenticity in naturalistic evaluation. *New directions for program evaluation,* (30), 73-84.

Levy, B. J., McVeigh, N. D., Marful, A., & Anderson, M. C. (2007). Inhibiting your native language: The role of retrieval-induced forgetting during second-language acquisition. *Psychological Science, 18*(1), 29-34. https://doi.org/10.1111/j.1467-9280.2007.01844.x

Lohr, M. (2000). New approaches to lexicostatistics and glottochronology. *Time Depth in Historical Linguistics, 1,* 209-222.

Lowe, J. B., & Mazaudon, M. (1994). The reconstruction engine: A computer implementation of the comparative method. *Computational Linguistics, 20*(3), 381-417.

Lynch, F., & Clotet, J. M. (1967). The Bukidnon of North-Central Mindanao in 1889. *Philippine Studies,* 15, 464–482. https://doi.org/10.2307/42720220

Magno, J. M. (2017). Oral interlanguages of second language (L2) learners of Filipino and English. *Asia Pacific Journal of Education, Arts and Sciences, 4*(2), 60–67.

Marian, V., & Spivey, M. (2003). Competing activation in bilingual language processing: Within-and between-language competition. *Bilingualism: Language and Cognition, 6*(2), 97-115.

Matras, Y. (2009). *Language contact.* Cambridge, UK. Cambridge University Press.

Melamed, I. D. (1999). Bitext maps and alignment via pattern recognition. *Computational Linguistics, 25*(1), 107-130.

Miller, F. G., Wendler, D., & Swartzman, L. C. (2005). Deception in research on the placebo effect. *PLoS Medicine, 2*(9), e262.

Miller, W. R. (1984). The classification of the Uto-Aztecan languages based on lexical evidence. *International Journal of American Linguistics, 50*(1), 1-24.

Nelson, H. (2001). Lexicostatistics Applied to the Historical Development of Three Languages of the Philippines. In *Deseret Language and Linguistic Society Symposium* (Vol. 27, No. 1, p. 7). Retrieved from https://scholarsarchive.byu.edu/dlls/vol27/iss1/7%0AThis

Newman, P. (1995). *On being right: Greenberg's African linguistic classification and the methodological principles which underlie it.* Bloomington, IN: Institute for the Study of Nigerian Languages and Cultures, Indiana University.

Nordquist, R. (2018). *Free variation in phonetics.* Retrieved from https://www.thoughtco.com/free-variation-phonetics-1690780

O'Brien, A. J. (2008). Conflict of interest in research. *The American Journal of Emergency Medicine, 26*(4), 504.https://doi.org/10.1016/j.ajem.2008.01.006

Ono, Y. (2019). The ordinal scale on lexicostatistical data in Ainu dialects: Towards a new interdisciplinary research among the humanities and statistics. *Northern Humanities Research, 12*, 89-110.

Oswalt, R. L. (1971). Towards the construction of a standard lexicostatistic list. *Anthropological Linguistics*, 421-434.

Patton, M. Q. (1990). *Qualitative evaluation and research methods.* Newbury Park, California. SAGE Publications, inc.

Patton, M. Q. (1999). Enhancing the quality and credibility of qualitative analysis. *Health Services Research, 34*(5 Pt 2), 1189.

Peng, A., & Billings, L. (2008). Binukid pronominal clisis. *Studies in Philippine Languages and Cultures, 17*, 179-212.

Posner, R. R., & Cremona, J. A. (1963). Romance linguistics. *The Year's Work in Modern Language Studies, 25*, 8-27.

Postholm, M. B., & Skrøvset, S. (2013). The researcher reflecting on her own role during action research. *Educational Action Research, 21*(4), 506-518.

Radford, A., Atkinson, M., Britain, D., Clahsen, H., & Spencer, A. (2009). *Linguistics: An introduction.* Cambridge, UK. Cambridge University Press.

Ringe, D. A. (1992). On calculating the factor of chance in language comparison. *Transactions of the American Philosophical Society, 82*(1), 1-110.

Rossi, E., & Diaz, M. (2016). How aging and bilingualism influence language processing. *Linguistic Approaches to Bilingualism, 6*(1), 9-42.

Ruhlen, M. (1994). The origin of language: *Tracing the evolution of the mother tongue* (No. 401 R933-o). New York: Wiley.

Salkind, N. J. (Ed.). (2010). *Encyclopedia of research design* (Vol. 1). Newbury Park, California, USA. Sage.

Sankoff, D. (1970). On the rate of replacement of word-meaning relationships. *Language*, 564-569.

Seid, M., & Adigeh, Y. (2017). A lexicostatistical analysis of Nine Aari dialects. *ZENA-LISSAN (Journal of Academy of Ethiopian Languages and Cultures), 26*(1), 19-51.

Serva, M., & Petroni, F. (2008). Indo-European languages tree by Levenshtein distance. *EPL (Europhysics Letters), 81*(6), 68005.

Schmid, M. S. (2008). Defining language attrition. *Babylonia, 2*(08), 9-12.

Schmidt J. E., Herrgen J. (2011). Sprachdynamik. Eine Einführung in die moderne Regionalsprachenformschung. Berlin: Erich Schmidt Verlag; (Grundlagen der Germanistik 49). [Google Scholar]

Shaw, S., & Barrett, G. (2006). Research governance: Regulating risk and reducing harm? *Journal of the Royal Society of Medicine, 99*(1), 14–19. https://doi.org/10.1258/jrsm.99.1.14

Shosted, R. (2000). Romani roots: A lexicostatistical analysis of Romani Hindustani, and Czech. In *Deseret Language and Linguistic Society Symposium* (Vol. 26, No. 1, p. 3). Retrieved from https://scholarsarchive.byu.edu/

Simons, G. F., & Fennig, C. D. (2018). Ethnologue: Languages of the world, twenty. *Dallas, Texas: SIL International. Online version: http://www.ethnologue. com Accessed, 26*(12), 2018.

Stake, R. E. (1994). Case study: Composition and performance. *Bulletin of the Council for Research in Music Education*, 31-44.

Starostin, S. (2000). Comparative-historical linguistics and lexicostatistics. *Time Depth in Historical Linguistics, 1*, 223-265.

Starostin, G. (2017). Lexicostatistical studies in East Sudanic I: On the genetic unity of Nubian-Nara-Tama. *Вестник РГГУ. Серия: Филология. Вопросы языкового родства*, (2), 87-113.

Sumbalan, A. T., Mirasol Jr, F. S., Mordeno, H. M. C., & Canoy, M. E. S. (2001). *Talamdan–Views on Mount Kitanglad, Philippines*. Retrieved from https://talamdan.wordpress.com/category/talamdan/2001/

Suminguit, V. J., Burton, E., & Canoy, E. (2001). A study on ancestral domain recognition and management within and around the Mt. Kitanglad Range National Park. In *Conference on Protected Area Management in the Philippines. Davao City. November* (pp. 12-16). Retrieved from http://www.worldagroforestry.org/

Swadesh, M. (1950). Salish internal relationships. *International Journal of American Linguistics, 16*(4), 157-167.

Swadesh, M. (1952). Lexico-statistic dating of prehistoric ethnic contacts: With special reference to North American Indians and Eskimos. *Proceedings of the American Philosophical Society, 96*(4), 452-463.

Swadesh, M. (1955). Towards greater accuracy in lexicostatistic dating. *International Journal of American linguistics, 21*(2), 121-137.

Tadmor, U., Haspelmath, M., & Taylor, B. (2010). Borrowability and the notion of basic vocabulary. *Diachronica, 27*(2), 226-246.

Thomas, B. (2000). National geographic, PANAMIN and the stone-age tribe. *Dialectical Anthropology, 25*(1), 77-88.

Thomas, D., & Healy, A. (1962). Some Philippine language subgroupings: A lexicostatistical study. *Anthropological Linguistics*, 21-33. https://doi.org/10.2307/30022390

Thurmond, V. A. (2001). The point of triangulation. *Journal of Nursing Scholarship, 33*(3), 253-258.

Tobin, G. A., & Begley, C. M. (2004). Methodological rigour within a qualitative framework. *Journal of Advanced Nursing, 48*(4), 388-396.

Trudgill P. (1986). *Dialects in Contact*. Oxford: Basil Blackwell; (Language and Society 10). [Google Scholar]

Urreiztieta-Rivera, I. (1980). Basque and Caucasian: A survey of the methods used in establishing ancient genetic affiliations. Retrieved from https://repository.arizona.edu/handle/10150/290541

Välimaa-Blum, R. (2005). Cognitive phonology in construction grammar: *Analytic tools for students of English*. Berlin, Germany: Walter de Gruyter.

Verhaeghen, P. (2003). Aging and vocabulary score: A meta-analysis. *Psychology and Aging, 18*(2), 332.

Wang W. S.-Y., Lien C. (1993). Bidirectional diffusion in sound change, in Historical Linguistics. Problems and Perspectives, ed Jones C., editor. (London; New York, NY: Longman;), 345–400. [Google Scholar]

Weinreich, U. (1953). Languages in contact, the Hague: Mouton. *Versión espa nola: Lenguas en contacto, trad. de F. Rivera, Caracas: Universidad Central de Venezuela, 1*, 974.

Wichmann, S., Müller, A., Velupillai, V., Brown, C. H., Holman, E. W., Brown, P., ... & Wett, A. (2010). The ASJP database (version 16). URL: http:// email. eva. mpg. de/~ wichmann/ASJPHomePage. htm, 3.

Wichmann, S., & Rama, T. (2018). 4. Jackknifing the Black Sheep: ASJP Classification Performance and Austronesian. *Senri Ethnological Studies, 98*, 39-58.

William, S. Y. W., & Lien, C. (2014). Bidirectional diffusion in sound change. *Historical Linguistics: Problems and perspectives*, 345.

Wimbish, J. (1986). The languages of the Zambales mountains: A Philippine lexicostatistic study. *Work Papers of the Summer Institute of Linguistics, University of North Dakota Session, 30*(1), 8.

Wolfenden, E. P. (1972). *A description of Hiligaynon phrase and clause constructions* (Doctoral dissertation, [Honolulu]). Retrieved from scholarspace.manoa.hawaii.edu

Yavas, M. S. (2006). *Applied English phonology*. New Jersey, USA. Blackwell Pub.

Zhang, M., & Gong, T. (2016). How many is enough?-Statistical principles for Lexicostatistics. *Frontiers in Psychology, 7*, 1916. https://doi.org/10.3389/fpsyg.2016.01916

Zietman, A. L. (2013). Falsification, fabrication, and plagiarism: The unholy trinity of scientific writing. *International Journal of Radiation Oncology• Biology• Physics, 87*(2), 225-227. https://doi.org/10.1016/j.ijrobp.2013.07.004

Zsiga, E. C. (2012). *The sounds of language: An introduction to phonetics and phonology*. New Jersey, USA. John Wiley & Sons.